MAIMONIDES ON HUMAN PERFECTION

Program in Judaic Studies
Brown University
BROWN JUDAIC STUDIES
Edited by
Jacob Neusner
Wendell S. Dietrich, Ernest S. Frerichs, William Scott Green,
Calvin Goldscheider, David Hirsch, Alan Zuckerman

Project Editors (Projects)

David Blumenthal, Emory University (Approaches to Medieval Judaism)
William Brinner (Studies in Judaism and Islam)
Ernest S. Frerichs, Brown University (Dissertations and Monographs)
Lenn Evan Goodman, University of Hawaii (Studies in Medieval Judaism)
William Scott Green, University of Rochester (Approaches to Ancient Judaism)
Norbert Samuelson, Temple University (Jewish Philosophy)
Jonathan Z. Smith, University of Chicago (Studia Philonica)

Number 202
MAIMONIDES ON HUMAN PERFECTION

by
Menachem Kellner

MAIMONIDES ON HUMAN PERFECTION

by

Menachem Kellner

Scholars Press
Atlanta, Georgia

MAIMONIDES ON HUMAN PERFECTION

BM
546
.K46
1990

© 1990
Brown University

Library of Congress Cataloging in Publication Data

Kellner, Menachem Marc, 1946-
    Maimonides on human perfection / by Menachem Kellner
    p. cm. -- (Brown Judaic studies ; no. 202)
    Includes bibliographical references.
    ISBN 1-55540-437-5 (alk. paper)
    1. Maimonides, Moses, 1135-1204--Views on perfection.
2. Perfection--Religious aspects--Judaism. 3. Judaism--Doctrines.
I. Title. II. Series.
BM546.K46 1990
296.3'2--dc20   89-48211
                                     CIP

Printed in the United States of America
on acid-free paper

For

Abraham and Rose Shoulson

Parents-in-Love

Contents

EDITOR'S FOREWORD

This volume inaugurates Studies in Medieval Judaism, a new series in Brown Judaic Studies. Its author, my friend and colleague, Menachem Kellner, is well known for his scholarly papers, his learned translation of the *Rosh Amanah* of Isaac Abravanel, his anthology on Contemporary Jewish Ethics, and, most recently, his extensive study of dogma in Jewish theology. The present monograph is a carefully researched and closely argued essay in the interpretation of Maimonides' conception of human perfection: How does Maimonides situate himself *vis a vis* the intellectual and the moral conceptions of human fulfillment? Given that Maimonides argues that our highest and most distinctively human attainments are intellectual, is it true that Maimonides identifies the philosopher as the highest type of human being, or does Maimonides set out still higher goals for those who attain intellectual perfection?

Charting his course among the carefully phrased texts of Maimonides' own exposition, Kellner argues that there clearly is a higher goal, to which intellectual perfection is necessary (just as moral perfection is necessary to our intellectual fulfillment), but that the idea of that higher goal is not adequately captured in the merely political or moral formulations assigned to it by scholars like Strauss, Pines, and Berman on the one hand, or Cohen, Guttmann and Schwarzschild on the other. The presence of Al-Farabi looms too large in the first instance, and that of Kant in the second, to allow the emergence of what is distinctively Jewish and indeed distinctively Maimonidean in Maimonides, Kellner argues. For the content that

Maimonides assigns to the moral and indeed political life of the intellectually perfected Jew derives from the *mitzvot*.

Developing a line of interpretation championed among our contemporaries by Twersky and Hartman, Kellner shows that the moral and political reductions of the Maimonidean ideal reflect a comparable theological reduction. His reading of the texts on human perfection can therefore cast some light on the Maimonidean idea of God as Creator and Source of revelation. And his admission that the Maimonidean ideal is not simply a reaffirmation of "orthodoxy" may shed light in turn on our conception of the commandments. For, as I have argued, Maimonides' idea of the commandments is militantly opposed to the notion of their pure positivity, without reason, theme, purpose or transcendent goal. To recognize that the commandments are the core and constitution of a moral and political system is not only to accord recognition to the commandments but also to understand their underlying basis and the principle of their historic growth, present application, and future elaboration.

Kellner's study is thus an important step in our resynthesizing the unity of Maimonidean thought, which has for too long been broken up prismatically to project only the varying refractivities or sensibilities of those who study it. In aiding us towards a larger and more inclusive synthesis, Kellner does more than aid the reputation of one of our greatest minds. He aids us as well in recementing our own consciousness, which the events of twenty centuries—and the last of those twenty certainly most traumatically—have done so much to shatter. He aids us in the recovery of our philosophic consciousness as Jews. For it is not only lives and populations that can be casualties of history and will require generations of peace to heal.

The present volume is a helpful one to us in delineating the focus of the series it inaugurates. This series is intended to be philosophical in the broad sense that it is founded on a community of intellectual interest in life and experience. Our matter is medieval, but the interest which I hope the series will bring to its historical matter will be lively, in the sense that it will foster living dialogue with the creative minds of our past. For we have much to learn from them if we study their works and ponder the problems they addressed in a spirit of candor and critical open mindedness. Other volumes are already in train, and scholars who have written original monographs that come within the purview of the series are invited and encouraged to submit their MSS. The standards of selection and editorial review will be as rigorous as we can make them (and there is blind external review), but the prize is participation in a philosophic discourse with an ancient and noble lineage and a future that is only beginning.

We owe thanks to Jacob Neusner for the aegis under which this series will appear, and to Menachem Kellner for boldly and smartly taking the first step.

L. E. Goodman, D. Phil.
Honolulu

Preface

This study is an examination of Maimonides' statements on the nature of human perfection. It takes as its starting point or orientation the claim that Maimonides took with ultimate seriousness the traditional Jewish assertion that God revealed the Torah through Moses to the Jewish People at Sinai. In other words, I start from the perspective that Maimonides held that God, for His own inscrutable reasons, really and truly commanded the *mizvot* for all Jews, both the perfected among them and the unperfected. But, as much as I start from that perspective, I also attempt to support it, to show that Maimonides' statements on human perfection make the most sense if they are interpreted in the light of this claim.

This study had its origins in an invitation to participate in a conference on Neoplatonism and Jewish Thought held at the University of Hawaii in Honolulu in December of 1987 under the auspices of the International Society for Neoplatonic Studies and organized by Professor Lenn Evan Goodman of the University of Hawaii. I would like to thank my colleagues at the conference, particularly Lenn Goodman, for their comments on my presentation there, comments which helped in the preparation of this study.

Lenn Goodman, editor of the series in which this study appears, went over the manuscript with great care and shared unstintingly his erudition, linguistic competence, and fine philosophic sophistication. For his generous assistance I am deeply grateful. Disagreements, of course, remain between us, and the responsibility for what lies before the reader is entirely my own. Additionally, I benefited from the insights of Steven Schwarzschild, who will always remain my teacher, Daniel Lasker, Yizhak Gross, and Abraham Melamed. To them all, my sincere thanks.

As this book was being prepared for press I received the sad news of the passing of Lawrence V. Berman of Stanford University, a painstaking and prolific scholar, with whom I carry on an extended and sometimes lively debate in this book. My disagreements with Berman about the proper interpretation of Maimonides are deep, but no deeper than my profound respect for him. *Yehi Zikhro Barukh.*

This monograph represents the first step in an extended project dealing with the question of human perfection in medieval Jewish thought. The next major step in this project will be an edition, translation, and analysis of Gersonides' commentary on Song of Songs which I hope to lay before the scholarly public in the near future.

Grateful acknowledgement is hereby made to the Memorial Foundation for Jewish Culture for a grant which supported the research on which this study is based. My thanks also to the Research Authority at the University of Haifa and especially to Mrs. Danielle Friedlander, for generous and cheerful technical assistance.

For technical reasons, Hebrew and Arabic terms are transliterated without diacritical marks.

Mt. Carmel
Haifa
Shavuot, 5749

Chapter One

Human Perfection as Intellectual Perfection

In examining Moses Maimonides' statements concerning the nature of human perfection we find that he appears to present two different accounts of the *summum bonum*. According to the first of these accounts, Maimonides maintains that humanity's highest perfection is perfection of the intellect. Maimonides takes this stand in texts scattered throughout his popular, halakhic, and philosophical writings.

In his non-philosophical writings, Maimonides nowhere explicitly states that humankind's highest perfection is intellectual. Rather, he implies it by making immortality a function of intellectual perfection. Thus, in Maimonides' earliest major work, his *Commentary on the Mishnah*, we find him commenting on the rabbinic statement, "in the world to come there is no eating, drinking, washing, annointing, or sexual intercourse; but the righteous sit with their crowns on their heads enjoying the radiance of the divine presence;"[1] he writes:

> The intent of the statement, 'their crowns on their heads,' is the existence of the soul through the existence of that which it knows,[2] in that they are the same thing,[3] as the experts in philosophy have maintained.[4]

The righteous reach the world to come, in other words, thanks to their knowledge of God.

We find similar ideas in Maimonides' great halakhic code, the *Mishneh Torah*. In "Laws of the Foundations of the Torah," IV 9, Maimonides explains why the soul survives the death of the body:

> This form of the soul[5] is not compounded of elements into which it would again dissolve. Nor does it exist by the energy of the vital principle, so that the latter would be necessary to its existence, in the way that the vital principle requires a physical body for its existence. But it comes directly from God in Heaven. Hence, when the material portion of our being dissolves into its component elements, and physical life perishes —since that only exists in association with the body and needs the body for its functions— this form of the Soul, is not destroyed, as it does not require physical life for its activities. It knows and apprehends the Intelligences that exist without material substance; it knows the Creator of All Things; and it endures for ever. . . .[6]

In this text again we learn that the soul can survive the destruction of the body by virtue of that which it knows. This may be phrased more formally as follows: only the acquired intellect survives the death of the body, and one achieves an acquired intellect only through cognition of God and the Separate Intellects.[7]

In a text emphasizing the spiritual character of life in the world to come, Maimonides stresses the connection between perfection of the intellect and the attainment of that life:

> In the world to come, there is nothing corporeal, and no material substance; there are only the souls of the righteous without bodies—like the ministering angels. . . . the phrase 'their crowns on their heads' refers to the knowledge they have acquired, and on account of which they have attained life in the world to come.[8]

Maimonides tells us once again, citing the same text he cited in his *Commentary on the Mishnah*, that one's portion in the world to come depends upon one's intellectual attainments. Here, however, he does not make clear what sort of intellectual attainments are necessary.

In "Laws of Moral Qualities," III 2 Maimonides urges: "A man should direct all his thoughts and activities to the knowledge of God alone. . . ." He goes on to emphasize that all our actions —eating and marital relations included— should be directed to this end.

Finally, in explaining the importance of observing the laws of the *mezuzah*, Maimonides says that when seeing it, one "will know that nothing endures for ever and ever but knowledge of the Rock of the Universe. . . ."[9] Seeing the *mezuzah* attached to our doorpost, then, has the salutory effect of reminding us that nothing in the world is of ultimate worth but attaining knowledge of God.

Further evidence of Maimonides' interpretation of human perfection in intellectualist terms in the *Mishneh Torah* can be found in the last two, messianic chapters of the work. The raison d'être of the messianic era, and its defining characteristic, is to spread the knowledge of God throughout the world.

In the four texts before us, then, Maimonides clearly states that attaining a share in the world to come, achieving immortality, depends upon a certain type of intellectual perfection that comes from acquiring true knowledge of God. If we can allow ourselves the safe assumption that for Maimonides immortality is achieved only by those who have perfected themselves, we may then say that Maimonides defines the peak of human perfection in intellectual terms. This is not to say that there are no other perfections or that intellectual perfection can be achieved without other, ancillary perfections, but, rather, that the highest perfection to which humans can aspire is defined in terms of the intellect.

Maimonides' claim is, to put it mildly, unusual in the context of rabbinic Judaism, the context of the halakhic works with which we have been dealing. And it is remarkable that he makes the claim so clearly and so often in a work addressed in the first instance to rabbis. The claim that the *summum bonum* consists in perfection of the intellect and that such perfection constitutes the necessary and sufficient condition for attaining a share in the world to come goes against the grain of rabbinic Judaism, with its emphasis on perfection through observance of God's commands and on purity of motive. This position found its classic expression in the well-known dictum, "study is not the main thing, but action."[10] For Maimonides, as Shlomo Pines notes, there is no room for "saintly simplicity" of the sort approved of, if not necessarily prized by, the Rabbis.[11] The unusual —one is tempted to say, heterodox— character of this doctrine makes its explicit repetitions in the *Mishneh Torah* remarkable.

In the *Guide of the Perplexed* Maimonides makes the claim that humankind's highest perfection resides in perfection of the intellect. He further claims that human immortality depends upon intellectual perfection. Near the beginning of the *Guide* Maimonides says that man's "ultimate perfection" is "the intellect that God caused to emanate unto man" (I 2, p. 24).

In discussing the term "to eat" in *Guide* I 30, Maimonides notes that it is applied figuratively "to knowledge, learning, and, in general, the intellectual apprehensions through which the permanence of the human form endures in the most perfect of states, just as the body endures through food in the finest of its states."[12] Perfection and permanent endurance (i.e., immortality), then, are consequences of "intellectual apprehensions."

In III 8 (p. 432), Maimonides maintains that one "should take as his end that which is the end of man qua man: namely, solely the mental representation[13] of the intelligibles, the most certain and the noblest of which being the apprehension, in as far as this is possible, of the deity, of the angels, and of His other works. These individuals are those who are permanently with God. . . .This is what is required of man; I mean to say that this is his end." The end of man, therefore, and that which is required of him, and that which enables him to be permanently with God, is the conception of the intelligibles.

In III 27 (p. 511), Maimonides writes that man's

> ultimate perfection[14] is to become rational in actu; this would consist in his knowing everything concerning all the beings that it is within the capacity of man to know in accordance with his ultimate perfection. It is clear that to this ultimate perfection there do not belong either actions or moral qualities and that it consists only of ideas toward which speculation has led and that investigation has rendered compulsory. It is also clear that this noble and ultimate perfection can only be achieved after the first perfection [the welfare of the body] has been achieved. For a man cannot represent to himself an intelligible even when taught to understand it and all the more cannot become aware of it on his own accord, if he is in pain or is very hungry or is thirsty or is hot or is very cold. But once the first perfection has been achieved it is possible to achieve the ultimate, which is indubitably more noble and is the only cause of permanent preservation.

In the following chapter (III 28, p. 512), we are informed that it is sound ideas "through which perfection may be obtained."

Much of chapter III 51 (to which we will return in some detail below) is given over to emphasizing and elaborating the theme "that that intellect which emanated from Him, may He be exalted, toward us is the bond between us and Him" (p. 621). It is in this chapter that Maimonides presents his famous parable of the palace with its clearly intellectualist stance (pp. 618-620) and links worship and providence to intellectual attainments.

Maimonides concludes the chapter with a stirring and impassioned appeal:

> The philosophers have explained that the bodily faculties impede in youth the attainment of most of the moral virtues, and all the more those of pure thought, which is achieved through the perfection of the intelligibles that lead to passionate love of Him, may He be exalted. For it is impossible that it should be achieved while the bodily humors are in effervescence. Yet in the measure in which the faculties of the body are weakened and the fires of the desires quenched, the intellect is strengthened, its lights achieve a wider extension, its apprehension is purified, and it rejoices in what it apprehends. The result is that when a perfect man is stricken with years and approaches death, this apprehension increases very powerfully, joy over this apprehension and a great love for the object of apprehension become stronger, until the soul is separated from the body at that moment in this state of pleasure. Because of this the Sages have indicated with reference to the deaths of Moses, Aaron, and Miriam that the three of them died by a

kiss. . . .Their purpose was to indicate that the three of them died in the pleasure of this apprehension due to the intensity of passionate love. . . . After having reached this condition of enduring permanence, that intellect remains in one and the same state, the impediment that sometime screened him off having been removed.[15] And he will remain permanently in that state of intense pleasure, which does not belong to the genus of bodily pleasures, as we have explained in our compilations and as others explained before us.[16]

Maimonides summarized this impassioned statement of *amor Dei intellectualis* in the clearest   terms in the last chapter of the *Guide*. Discussing the four species of perfections found in humankind, Maimonides states:

> The fourth kind is the true human perfection; it consists in the acquisition of the rational virtues—I refer to the conception of intelligibles, which teach true views concerning metaphysics. This is in true reality the ultimate end; this is what gives the individual true perfection, a perfection belonging to him alone; and it gives him permanent perdurance; through it man is man. If you consider each of the three perfections mentioned before, you will find that they pertain to others than you, not to you, even though, according to the generally accepted opinion, they inevitably pertain both to you and to others. This ultimate perfection, however, pertains to you alone, no one else being associated in it with you in any way: *They shall be thine own*, and so on.[17] Therefore, you ought to desire to achieve this thing, which will remain permanently with you, and not weary and trouble yourself for the sake of other things. . . .[18]

The conception of intelligibles, then, which teach true views concerning the divine things, is the true human perfection. It is the ultimate end for human beings and gives them true perfection; through it one achieves one's true end as a human being. It is the ultimate perfection, the only truly human perfection, the only truly worthy object of our desires.[19]

This interpretation of Maimonides' conception of human perfection has been adopted by many of his interpreters.[20] This is hardly surprising, given the explicit and emphatic way in which Maimonides teaches this doctrine in the *Commentary on the Mishnah*, in the *Mishneh Torah*, and in the *Guide of the Perplexed*. This is, however, an interpretation which must be rejected.

Chapter Two

Human Perfection as Practical Perfection

Maimonides, as is well-known, contradicts himself on more than one occasion in the *Guide*. Indeed, in his introduction to that work, he warns the reader that there are two types of contradictions in the *Guide*. The first is of a pedagogical nature: it is occasionally necessary for a teacher to be "lax" and "not undertake to state the matter as it truly is in exact terms" until the student is better prepared. This is the fifth of seven causes of contradiction which Maimonides analyzes. The seventh, which is the second type of contradiction to be found in the *Guide*, is phrased as follows:

> In speaking about very obscure matters it is necessary to conceal some parts and to disclose others. Sometimes in the case of certain dicta this necessity requires that the discussion proceed on the basis of a certain premise, whereas in another place necessity requires that the discussion proceed on the basis of another premise contradicting the first one. In such cases the vulgar must in no way be aware of the contradiction; the author accordingly uses some device to conceal it by all means (p. 18).

Maimonides has long been interpreted as maintaining here that he has an esoteric doctrine in the *Guide* which he wishes to keep hidden from the masses.[1]

Granted that Maimonides contradicts himself, rarely does he do it in so blatant a fashion as with the issue of human perfection. In the very chapter of the *Guide* in which we find Maimonides' explicit summation of his doctrine that for human beings true and ultimate perfection is apprehension of the intelligibles, we find his surprising exposition of Jeremiah 9:22-23.[2] The verses read as follows:

> Thus saith the Lord: Let not the wise man glory in his wisdom, neither let the mighty man glory in his might, let not the rich man glory in his riches; but let him that glorieth glory in this, that he understandeth and knoweth Me, that I am the Lord who exercise loving-kindness, judgment, and righteousness in the earth; for in these things I delight, saith the Lord.

Jeremiah, Maimonides maintains, while explaining "the noblest ends" does not "limit them only to the apprehension of Him, may He be exalted." Rather, he says "that one should glory in the apprehension of

7

Myself and in the knowledge of My attributes, by which he means His actions" (III 54, p. 637). We are to imitate God's providential actions. Maimonides expresses this clearly in the penultimate paragraph of the *Guide*:

> It is clear that the perfection of man that may truly be gloried in is the one acquired by him who has achieved, in a measure corresponding to his capacity, apprehension of Him, may He be exalted, and who knows His providence extending over His creatures as manifested in the act of bringing them into being and their governance as it is. The way of life of such an individual, after he has achieved this apprehension, will always have in view *loving-kindness*, *righteousness*, and *judgment*, through assimilation to His actions, may He be exalted, just as we have explained several times in this Treatise. (p. 638)

What we appear to have here is a dramatic shift in Maimonides' thinking. No longer is apprehension of God man's most glorious perfection. The most "perfect perfection" is that of the individual who not only knows God, but understands the ways of God's providence and strives to imitate those ways in his or her actions. The *vita activa* appears to be the ideal, and not the *vita contemplativa*.

In light of Maimonides' statements here at the very end of the Guide, many modern interpreters of his thought have been moved to reject the purely intellectualist account of Maimonides' position on human perfection and supplement it or replace it with accounts which take note of the active form of *imitatio Dei* which Maimonides seems to call for in the texts just cited. Two schools of thought have developed in this connection. The first, represented by such thinkers as Hermann Cohen, Julius Guttmann, and Steven Schwarzschild, maintains that for Maimonides the ultimate form of human perfection is the imitation of God's moral qualities.[3] The second, represented by interpreters such as Leo Strauss, Lawrence Berman, and Shlomo Pines (whose position on this issue has undergone radical development over the years), maintains that for Maimonides the ultimate form of human perfection is the imitation of God's governance of the world through the creation of just states.[4] If the first school sees human perfection in moral terms, the second sees it in political terms.

In his essay, "The Character of Maimonides' Ethics,"[5] Hermann Cohen maintains that "love of God means morality which is God's essence" (p. 41). Cohen's position is based upon a detailed reading of Maimonides' theory of divine attributes, a reading which leads Cohen to the conclusion that Maimonides denies that there is any distinction between God's will and God's intellect. God's will (for human beings) is then defined in terms of moral behavior, "since morality is the divine substance as known [by human beings]" (p. 41).

This view is reiterated by Julius Guttmann, who wrote concerning Guide III 54 that "ethics, though previously subordinate to knowledge, has now become the ultimate meaning and purpose of God." Pointing up the connection between one's view of the nature of God and one's view of the nature of human perfection, a point to which we will have occasion to revert below, Guttmann continues, "While the God of Aristotle is still the supreme thought, and that of the Neoplatonist is the highest self-indwelling being, the God of Maimonides is a God of moral action."[6] Steven Schwarzschild has lately defended this position with verve and ingenuity, seeking to unite the intellectualist and moral accounts of human perfection. Since God is morality, Schwarzschild maintains, following Cohen, knowledge of God to the highest degree possible means knowledge of morality to the highest degree possible. It is a simple step to go from knowledge of morality to moral behavior, especially if one agrees with Socrates that virtue is knowledge.[7]

The most detailed account of the political interpretation of human perfection in Maimonides is found in a series of studies written by Lawrence V. Berman. Starting from the position originally suggested by Leo Strauss,[8] that Maimonides is, in effect, much more the disciple of Al-Farabi than of Moses, Berman imputes to Maimonides the position that God's governance of the world finds expression only in the constant, uninterrupted workings of the laws of nature. We are bound to imitate God but can hardly do so in terms of governing the world through laws of nature; we can do so, however, through the founding of the best possible state. The ultimate perfection of a human being, then, is to become a philosopher-prophet-king who founds a new state based upon the best principles of justice.

Shlomo Pines has recently supported Berman's thesis with a closely reasoned argument purporting to show that Maimonides actually held that intellectual perfection, at least in terms of apprehension of cognitive truths about God, cannot possibly be attained by human beings. This being so, and since "the only positive knowledge of God of which man is capable is knowledge of the attributes of action, and this leads and ought to lead to a sort of political activity which is the highest perfection of man, the practical way of life, the *bios praktikos*, is superior to the theoretical."[9]

Pines' position here is foreshadowed in his "Translator's Introduction." He maintains

> that Maimonides through his own activities was an exemplar of the Platonic philosopher-statesman. And this refers not only to *Mishneh Torah*, which codifies the Jewish law, and consequently constitutes an eminently political achievement, but also to the *Guide* itself, which, as its Introduction makes clear, is not comparable, either in its external and internal structure or in its objectives, to the exclusively theoretical, systematized treatises of the philosophers. To some degree at least, the purpose that Maimonides had in mind when writing the *Guide* may be fairly described as political. (p. lxxxix)

Part of that political goal (which Pines says "aimed both at the legitimation of prophetic religion from the philosophic point of view and of philosophy from the religious") relates to the need for religious beliefs:

> Maimonides had very strong convictions concerning the utility and even necessity of an official system of religious beliefs for the preservation of communal obedience to the law. What is more, he lived up to his convictions by formulating in his commentary on the Mishneh the thirteen principal dogmas of Judaism. (p. cxviii)

Yet another interpretation of Maimonides' conception of human perfection has been advanced of late by Isadore Twersky and David Hartman. Twersky writes, "Maimonides believed that knowledge stimulates and sustains proper prescribed conduct [i.e., obedience to halakhah] which in turn is a conduit for knowledge, and this intellectual achievement in return *raises* the level and motive of conduct."[10] Hartman makes substantially the same point: "The primacy of action is not weakened by the contemplative ideal; a deeper purpose for the normative structure is realized instead once the philosophic way is followed. The contemplative ideal is not insulated from halakhah, but affects it in a new manner. Sinai is not a mere stage in man's spiritual development, but the ultimate place to which man constantly returns —even when he soars to the heights of metaphysical knowledge."[11] The position advanced here boils down to the claim that while perfection of the intellect is surely to be prized above all other perfections, it is not in itself the final end of human existence but itself serves as a way of deepening, enriching, and elevating observance of the mizvot.

In the rest of this study, I propose to defend a version of this interpretation of Maimonides, indicating why it is superior to the other interpretations briefly described here. I am not going to prove that the "halakhic" interpretation of human perfection in Maimonides as I present it is correct and that the intellectualist, moral, and political interpretations are incorrect. In the first place, they are not entirely incorrect, as I will indicate. In the second place, I do not believe that such a proof is possible. Maimonides did too good a job of hiding his true views. The most that can be done is to put forward an interpretation of Maimonides that does as little violence as possible to the texts he left us and is as consistent as possible with everything we know of the man.

Chapter Three

Exposition of *Guide* III 51-54

Maimonides devotes twenty-six chapters of the third part of the *Guide* (III 25-50) to a discussion of law in general and the Torah in particular, the lion's share of his account being given over to explications of the reasons for the commandments.[1] The last four chapters of the *Guide*, which follow immediately upon this discussion, are traditionally considered together as a unit.[2] The point of the first of these chapters (III 51), as Maimonides tells us, is "to confirm men in the intention to set their thought to work on God alone after they have achieved knowledge of Him, as we have explained" (p. 620). The wording of this statement should draw our attention. Maimonides announces his intention of pursuing a practical end in this chapter, not a theoretical one. He is not engaging in philosophy or theology, however one may define those terms in the context of medieval culture; he is not involved in apologetics or polemics; he is, rather, seeking a purely *religious* end: to move human beings to worship God in the most appropriate way possible.[3] This fact cries out for explanation and alerts us to the fact that the chapter we are reading is unlike the other chapters in the *Guide*, given over as they are to explanations.[4] This practical emphasis, it should be noted, continues the orientation of chapters 25-50, which deal with the commandments of the Torah.

Maimonides opens III 51 as follows:

> This chapter that we bring now does not include additional matter over and above what is comprised in other chapters of this Treatise. It is only a kind of conclusion, at the same time explaining the worship practiced by one who has apprehended the true realities peculiar only to Him after he has obtained an apprehension of what He is; and it also guides him toward achieving this worship, which is the end of man, and makes known to him how providence watches over him in this habitation until he is brought over to the *bundle of life*. (p. 618)

Maimonides makes the following claims here: (a) there is nothing new in this chapter, it being a conclusion for the book as a whole;[5] (b) this chapter explains a particular kind of worship—the worship of an individual who first obtains an apprehension of what God is and then apprehends the true realities peculiar only to God; we are dealing here with a person who has achieved the pinnacle of intellectual perfection, knowing what there is to know, not only about God's actions (the world in which we live), and not only about the Separate Intellects, but about God Himself;[6] (c) the chapter not only describes this special worship but also guides the reader in his or her[7] attempts to achieve it—Maimonides, that is, aims to make his reader alter his or her practice; (d) this special worship is the end of humankind; (e) the chapter explains the special providence extended to the person who achieves this form of worship while he or she lives in this world before reaching the world to come.[8]

Maimonides then presents his famous "parable of the palace":

> The ruler is in his palace, and all his subjects are partly within the city and partly outside the city. Of those who are within the city, some have turned their backs upon the ruler's habitation, their faces being turned another way. Others seek to reach the ruler's habitation, turn toward it, and desire to enter it and stand before him, but up to now they have not yet seen the wall of the habitation. Some of those who seek to reach it have come up to the habitation and walk around it searching for its gate. Some of them have entered the gate and walk about in the antechambers. Some of them have entered the inner court of the habitation and have come to be with the king, in one and the same place with him, namely in the ruler's habitation. But their having come into the inner part of the habitation does not mean that they see the ruler or speak to him. For after their coming into the inner part of the habitation, it is indispensable that they should make another effort; then they will be in the presence of the ruler, see him from afar or from nearby, or hear the ruler's speech or speak to him. (p. 618)

Maimonides here divides all human beings into several categories, which he explains as follows:[9]

(a) Those outside the city. These, Maimonides explains, are individuals without doctrinal belief; they are creatures halfway between apes and humans.

(b) Those in the city facing away from the palace. These are individuals who have adopted incorrect doctrinal belief and the farther they walk, the farther they get from the palace. These are far worse than the first group and "necessity at certain times calls for killing them. . . ."

(c) Those who seek to enter the palace but have not yet seen it. These are the Jewish masses, "the ignoramuses who observe the commandments."

(d) Those who have reached the habitation and circle it, seeking a way in. These are halakhists who hold to the true beliefs or views but "who do not engage in speculation concerning the fundamental principles of religion and make no inquiry whatever regarding the rectification of belief." These individuals "are engaged in studying the mathematical sciences and the art of logic."

(e) Those who have entered the gate and walk around in the antechambers. These are those "who have entered into speculation concerning the fundamental principles of religion" and "understood the natural sciences."[10]

(f) Those who have entered the inner court of the palace and are there with the ruler. This is he[11] "who has achieved demonstration, to the extent that that is possible, of everything that may be demonstrated; and who has ascertained in divine matters, to the extent that that is possible, everything that may be ascertained; and who has come close to certainty in those matters in which one can only come close to it." These latter are "the men of science" who "are of different grades of perfection." One of those grades consists of those who, after attaining perfection in the study of metaphysics, "turn wholly toward God. . . .and direct all the acts of their intellect toward an examination of the beings with a view to drawing from them proof with regard to Him, so as to know his governance of them in whatever way it is possible."[12] These are the prophets. Another of these grades consists, apparently, of Moses, who "attained such a degree that it is said of him, *And he was there with the Lord.*" (Ex. 34:28)

This parable created more of a furor, perhaps, than any other passage in the *Guide.* Traditionally inclined readers of Maimonides were outraged at the implication that "men of science" attained a higher degree of perfection and closeness to God than the halakhists. Shem Tov, for example, makes the following comment:

> Shem Tov said: Many rabbinic scholars said Maimonides did not write this chapter and if he did write it, it ought to be hidden away or, most appropriately, burned. For how could he say that those who know natural matters [physics] are on a higher level than those who engage in religion, and even more that they are with the ruler in the inner chamber, for on this basis the philosophers who are engaged with physics and metaphysics have achieved a higher level than those who are immersed in Torah![13]

Shem Tov himself does not propose so radical a solution to the problem. He cites Efodi (from a text I have not been able to locate) as follows:

> When I was very young I saw a fitting commentary to this chapter in Efodi's Introduction, a commentary which dissolved the problem [and which

showed that] the rabbinic scholars neither knew nor understood this chapter. He said: Maimonides divided those who engage in the Torah into three types, paralleling three types who engage in science after each has reached the Palace. [I] The first division who reach the Palace and walk around it are the Talmudists who know the Torah by tradition and do not engage themselves in the study of the roots of commandments and [the] faith; corresponding are the scientists who have learned the mathematical sciences and logic. [II] He then mentioned the second type; these are the men of the Torah who have engaged in the study of the principles of religion, these being the foundations of the Torah mentioned by Maimonides in the "Laws of [the Foundations of the Torah" in the Book of] Knowledge." Concerning these he said that they have entered the antechamber and that "people there indubitably have different ranks." Paralleling them he made another division among the scientists about whom he said, "If, however, you have understood the natural things you have entered [the habitation and are walking in] the antechamber[s]." [III] He made a further division among the men of the Torah, those who engage in *Ma'aseh Merkavah* and also know *Ma'aseh Bereshit* and have reached the king inside the Palace. This is indicated by: " . . .he who has achieved demonstration. . . . in divine matters. . . ." Paralleling them he made a further division among the scientists about whom he said, "If, however, you have achieved perfection in the natural things and have understood divine science, you have entered into the ruler's place, into the inner court."

Efodi's solution rests upon the claim that Maimonides posits two parallel routes to perfection, one for scientists and one for Talmudists. A similar solution is offered by Falaquera:

This parable, which Maimonides wrote at the beginning of this chapter, is applicable to men who achieve perfection by their investigation of existents and their speculation upon them, but *the holy that are in the earth* [Psalms 16:3] achieve perfection and truth without learning the sciences of the scientists. For God guides him who wants His truth and teaches him [how] to be among those who come nigh unto Him. Divine perfection is achieved with divine assistance.[14]

Falaquera, unlike Efodi, seems to prize the religious route to perfection over the scientific; but for both of them, perfection is attainable through either route.

This problem, which so exercized Falaquera, Efodi, Shem Tov, and others is based, I want to show here, on a false reading of Maimonides. He nowhere implies that philosophers attain a higher degree of perfection than halakhists. In short, I propose a new interpretation of the parable of the palace, one that is consistent with the text, the context, and many other statements of Maimonides, in the *Guide* and in his other works. In proposing this interpretation, I reject those interpretations of Maimonides which see him in basically naturalist (or what we would call today secularist) terms, as a convinced philosopher of the Al-Farabian school who felt the need, for whatever reason, to pay lip service to the teachings of Judaism as ordinarily conceived.[15] Similarly, I reject the moral interpretation of human perfection in Maimonides, at least in the way in which it is ordinarily expressed.

The parable, as I understand it, deals with Jews only, at least from the third and possibly from the second class onward. There is simply no comparison drawn in the parable between Jews and non-Jews, or between halakhists and gentile philosophers. There is, rather, a comparison between halakhists plain and simple and halakhists who have perfected themselves in natural science and philosophy. Whatever Maimonides may have felt about the intellectual perfection of Aristotle and other philosophers, and about the chances of immortality for non-Jews, the issue does not come up in the parable of the palace.

The first group in the parable are subhumans, and certainly not Jews. They are "outside the city," though of course as creatures, still subjects of the ruler. These are "all human individuals who have no doctrinal belief, neither one based on speculation nor one that accepts the authority of tradition. . . ."

The second class is the first of those within the city; it consists of individuals who have adopted incorrect doctrinal beliefs. These people face away from the palace and the farther they walk, the farther they go from it. These people are far worse than the first group and from time to time they must be killed. Who are these people? I propose to answer that question by examining the writings of Maimonides, especially the *Mishneh Torah*, with an eye to determining whom "necessity at certain times" calls for us to kill.

The following groups are candidates for execution due to the incorrect beliefs which they hold: members of the seven nations,[16] inhabitants of a corrupted city,[17] those who corrupt individuals,[18] and certain classes of Jewish heretics.[19] Of these, only the seven nations are not Jewish. Are they, then, the seond group in the parable? Hardly: Maimonides explicitly tells us that the obligation to destroy the seven nations is no longer operative. After telling us that it is a positive obligation to destroy them, and the transgression of a negative commandment not to do so if it is in one's power, Maimonides adds: "But their memory has long perished."[20]

The importance of this addition is emphasized by the fact that in his discussion of the obligation to destroy *Amalek* in the next paragraph, Maimonides does not make such a statement.[21] Maimonides, thus, historicizes the obligation to destroy the seven nations. "Necessity," therefore, does not "at certain times" call for us to kill them, at least not any more.[22]

Were these the only groups which we are called upon to execute for their beliefs, we could then conclude with certainty that the members of the second class of the parable are all Jews. The situation, however, is not altogether clear. In "Laws of Kings," VIII 9, Maimonides asserts that "any heathen who refuses to accept these seven commandments[23] is put to death if he is under our control."[24] Now the seven Noahide commandments referred to here deal mostly with behavior and, as such, do not directly and immediately relate to correct or incorrect beliefs. Inasmuch, however, as one of the seven forbids idolatry, and inasmuch as heathens ought to obey these commandments because God "commanded them in His Law and made known through Moses, our teacher, that the observance thereof had been enjoined upon the descendents of Noah even before the Law was given,"[25] there are grounds for seeing the execution of heathens who refuse to accept the Noahide laws as an instance of putting non-Jews to death for their incorrect beliefs. This being so, it may be that the second category in the parable refers, not to heretical Jews, but to recalcitrant heathens.

We have seen that the third class of human beings discussed by Maimonides in his parable are "those who seek to reach the ruler's habitation. . . .but have not yet seen [its] wall." Maimonides characterizes these individuals as "the multitude of the adherents of the Law, I refer to the ignoramuses who observe the commandments." What we have here is the first group to face the palace in the parable and the first group of Jews mentioned in the parable, people who study and observe the halakhah but nothing more.

The next class, the fourth, is described as those who have found the habitation and circle it, "searching for its gate." These individuals are characterized by Maimonides as

> the jurists who hold true opinions on the basis of traditional authority and study the law concerning the practices of divine service, but do not engage in speculation concerning the fundamental principles of religion and make no inquiry whatever regarding the rectification of belief.

Such individuals are further characterized by Maimonides as being "engaged in studying mathematical sciences and the art of logic."[26] We have here a group of Jews, smaller than the previous one, and more sophisticated as well. These Jews are not "ignoramuses who observe the commandments"; they are "jurists"[27] who "believe true opinions," not on the basis of rational demonstration, but "on the basis of traditional authority." As such, they make no effort to understand or confirm their traditionally accepted beliefs. Their sophistication lies not only in the fact that in addition to observing halakhah, they also study it and accept true opinions. It lies also in the fact that they are familiar with mathematics and logic.

The following class, the fifth, "have entered the gate and walk about in the antechambers." These are individuals who, according to Maimonides, "have engaged in speculation concerning the fundamental principles of religion" and have "understood the natural sciences," i.e., physics. These individuals are of different ranks. As the parable is ordinarily understood, these individuals are thought to be scientists competent in physics but not in metaphysics. Such an interpretation, it seems clear to me, misrepresents Maimonides' intention here. The fifth class is indeed composed of individuals competent in physics, but these, I would argue, are *Talmudists* ("jurists," in Maimonides' language) competent in physics, not simply scientists. Maimonides is not comparing scientists and Talmudists here, to the detriment of the latter; rather, he is comparing scientifically trained Talmudists and Talmudists pure and simple, to the detriment of the latter. A number of considerations support this interpretation.

The parable is found at the beginning of chapter III 51, a chapter which follows immediately upon twenty-six chapters given over to explanations of the commandments. The immediate context of the parable, therefore, is defined in terms of Torah and commandments. It is not unreasonable to read III 51 as continuing this orientation. As we noted above, this chapter, usually cited as the height of Maimonidean intellectualism, actually has a practical orientation: to bring people to adopt certain modes of behavior. This practical orientation does not exclude the moral and political interpretations of human perfection in Maimonides; rather, it lends some small measure of support to all those interpretations —moral, political, and halakhic— which see Maimonides' vision of human perfection in practical as opposed to purely intellectual terms.

In the parable, we see an ever-narrowing focus on Jews from at least the third class on: the ignorant masses who observe the commandments, jurists who hold true opinions, and now, if I am right, those who speculate concerning the fundamental principles of religion. This can be made clearer by looking at the parable in table form. But first, let me note that, for reasons which will be adduced below, it is hardly credible to suppose that Maimonides seriously entertained the idea that gentiles would prophesy. Here is how the parable looks when set out in the form of a table:

Out of the City
1. subhumans without doctrine ....(gentile)
In the City, but facing away from the Palace
2. idolators...(unclear)
In the City and facing the Palace
3. Jewish masses...(Jewish)
4. jurists ....(Jewish)
5. speculate on the fundamentals of religion/study physics ......(?)
6. metaphysicians ....(?)
7. prophets of different grades...(Jewish)
8. Moses ....(Jewish)

The first group consists of human-like creatures without doctrines at all. Idolators, individuals with incorrect doctrines, make up the next group. The third group, the Jewish masses, is the first group of those who actually face the palace and seek the Ruler in the parable. The fourth class, the halakhists (jurists), is not only smaller than the third, but a subset of it. Skipping for a moment to the sixth group, we find that it is not only smaller than the fifth (many more people study the principles of religion and physics than study metaphysics), but a subset of it as well: all metaphysicians must be physicists, but not the reverse. Similarly, the seventh group is a subset of the sixth: all prophets must be metaphysicians, but not the reverse. This analysis can even be extended to the last level: it is reasonable to assume that Moses must have passed through the stage of "normal" prophecy on the way to the perfection which made him Moses. All Moseses, so to speak, therefore, must be "normal" prophets, but not the reverse.[28] Considerations of symmetry and order (well known to be important to Maimonides[29]) alone almost compel us to complete this picture by making the fifth group a subset of the fourth. Those who "have entered the gate and walk about the antechambers," therefore, those individuals who "have engaged in speculation concerning the fundamental principles of religion," and have "understood the natural sciences," are "the jurists who believe true opinions on the basis of traditional authority and study the law concerning the practice of divine service." They are, that is to say, Talmudists.

These considerations are supported by the fact that Maimonides constructs his parable in the form of concentric circles, the larger of which are, naturally, more inclusive than the smaller. This does not commit us to claiming that all Jews are ex-pagans, only that the Jews are a subset of the class of human beings; human beings, in turn, are a subset of the class of creatures having human form (the subhumans outside the city). In historical terms, Jews are, in fact, ex-pagans, as Maimonides makes clear in his account of Abraham's discovery of monotheism in "Laws of Idolatry," I. Each circle, then, is smaller than the one surrounding it and included in it. If the members of the fourth circle are Talmudically trained Jews, then the members of the fifth circle are also Talmudically trained Jews.

An interesting parallel is found between the fifth and fourth classes, which supports the contention that in important respects they are isomorphic. The fourth class consists of Jews who studied logic and mathematics and accepted the true opinions taught in the Torah. The fifth class consists of individuals who studied physics (the subject following logic and mathematics) and speculate concerning the principles of religion (i.e., do not simply accept them as true beliefs on the basis of traditional authority). The fifth class, it is reasonable to conclude, consists of individuals from the fourth class who have pursued further the studies originally undertaken when they were still in the fourth class. In short, the members of the fifth class, like the members of the fourth, are or at least were Talmudists.

Note that Maimonides defines the members of the fourth class as jurists who "do *not* engage in speculation concerning the fundamental principles of religion." In this they are contrasted with the members of the fifth class, who "*have* engaged in speculation concerning the fundamental principles of religion." The fact that Maimonides contrasts the two classes so clearly on this specific issue indicates that on other issues they have a lot in common. What they have in common, I submit, is that they are Talmudically trained Jews.

Maimonides characterizes the members of the fifth class as individuals who have studied physics and "engaged in speculation concerning the fundamental principles of religion." What does Maimonides mean here by "the fundamental principles of religion?" The Arabic term is *usul al-din*. Maimonides seems to use the terms *asl* (root or principle) and *qa'idah* (foundation) interchangeably.[30] What are the roots or foundations of religion? Maimonides calls his "Thirteen Principles" roots and foundations of the Torah in the text wherein they are introduced,[31] but he does not specifically call them roots or foundations of religion (*din*). Still, unless we are willing to admit that Maimonides accepted a category of true religions independent of Judaism,[32] a highly unlikely proposition, we may safely assume that he would not make a sharp distinction between the "principles of religion" and the "principles of Judaism," the latter, on his own evidence, being the "Thirteen Principles" introduced in his *Commentary on the Mishnah*.

Just as Maimonides uses two Arabic terms, *asl* and *qa'idah*, interchangeably, so he seems to use the two parallel Hebrew terms, *ikkar* and *yesod*, in the same manner.[33] He calls the first section of the *Mishneh Torah* "Laws of the Foundations [*yesodei*] of the Torah" and discusses there the following topics: God's existence, unity, and incorporeality, the structure of the physical universe, laws concerning the sanctification of God's name and its protection, prophecy, and Mosaic prophecy. If "*Hilkhot Yesodei ha-Torah*" is Maimonides' Hebrew version of *usul al-din*, then perhaps the contents of this text is an indication of what Maimonides means by "principles of religion." This is a reasonable interpretation, and is supported by other texts of Maimonides.

There are a number of places in the *Mishneh Torah* where Maimonides calls certain doctrines by the name *ikkar* (root or principle). In "Laws of the Foundations of the Torah," I 6, he calls belief in one God "the great *ikkar* upon which everything depends" (see also "Laws of Idolatry," I 2). Human freedom is called "a great *ikkar* and pillar of the Torah and commandment" in "Laws of Repentance," V 3 (see also VI 1). "The great *ikkar* upon which everything depends" is defined as God's unity, loving Him, and studying His [Torah] in "Laws of the Reading of the Sh'ma," I 2. Finally, and by far most importantly, in his discussion of conversion to Judaism in "Laws of Forbidden Intercourse," XIV 2, Maimonides defines *ikkarei ha-dat* (principles of religion = *usul al-din*) as "God's unity and the prohibition of idolatry." These two issues are, respectively, the second positive and first negative commandments in

Maimonides' listing of the commandments and appear at the very beginning of "Laws of the Foundations of the Torah" (I 1 and I 6). Here we have an explicit statement to the effect that, at least at this stage of his career and in this context, Maimonides defined the principles of religion in terms of God's unity and the prohibition of idolatry.

Whereas the terms *asl* and *qa'idah* appear in connection with a wide variety of doctrines in the *Guide*, in only one place does Maimonides make reference to *usul al-din*, and that is here in the text under discussion. With very few exceptions, all the other references to roots or foundations refer to doctrines included in Maimonides' "Thirteen Principles."[34]

Maimonides makes a further reference to *usul al-din* in his *Medical Aphorisms*. He cites a composition of his own on the *usul al-din*.[35] It is not clear when *Medical Aphorisms* was written. J. Kafih maintains that this work was written before the *Guide*.[36] If he is correct, then it is most appropriate to assume that by a composition on "the principles of religion," Maimonides meant his "Thirteen Principles." L. V. Berman, however, holds that this text was written after the *Guide* and that the composition on "the principles of religion" is the *Guide* itself.[37] If Kafih is correct, then we see Maimonides using the term *usul al-din* with reference to his "Thirteen Principles." If Berman is correct, then we see Maimonides using the term with reference to the *Guide*. Either way the term refers to explicitly *Jewish* works.[38]

To summarize, the textual evidence we have been able to adduce shows that Maimonides most probably meant one or more of the following things by his term "principles of religion": (a) the "Thirteen Principles"; (b) the "Laws of the Foundations of the Torah"; (c) the doctrines of God's unity, human freedom, love of God, and that there are no other gods; (d) the teachings of the *Book of Knowledge*; (e) various doctrines taught in the *Guide* (most of which appear in the "Thirteen Principles" and all of which appear in one place or another in the *Mishneh Torah*); and (f) the Jewish teachings taken up in the *Guide*. The important point here is that these issues are all dealt with in specifically *Jewish* works, all of which are aimed at Talmudists. This most emphatically includes the *Guide*, addressed explicitly as it is to perplexed Talmudists of a speculative bent. Thus, we have a further reason for understanding the individuals who comprise the fifth class as *Jewish* jurists (i.e., Talmudists) who have "engaged in speculation concerning the fundamental principles of religion."

Maimonides himself insists in the *Mishneh Torah* that the study of physics and metaphysics is the proper completion of Talmudic training. His statements on this matter have been subjected to incisive and convincing analysis by Isadore Twersky and there is no point in repeating the analysis here.[39] For our purposes it is sufficient to note that the fact that Maimonides saw in the study of physics and metaphysics the proper completion of Talmudic training lends credence to my claim that the members of the fifth class in the parable are Talmudists who go on to master physics and the principles of religion, and not the scientifically trained non-Talmudists, as has traditionally been thought to be the case.

Maimonides, as we have noted again and again, characterizes the members of the fifth class in the parable as individuals who have "entered into speculation concerning the fundamental principles of religion" and have "understood the natural sciences." In contrast to them, it is the members of the sixth class who have achieved some measure of perfection in metaphysics. This presents us with a problem. In the traditional interpretation of the parable, how are we to understand the "fundamental principles of religion" about which the members of the fifth class speculate? If we take them to be the *philosophical* proofs of God's existence, unity, and incorporeality, then we are treading in the field of metaphysics, which takes us into the sixth category. It is Maimonides himself, after all, who, in the *Mishneh Torah*, explains the term *ikkarei ha-dat* (*usul al-din* = principles of religon) in terms of God's existence and the prohibition of idolatry.[40] Now, since the "principles of religion" studied by the members of the fifth group cannot be *philosophical* proofs of God's existence, unity, and incorporeality (the philosophical way of expressing belief in God's existence and the prohibition of idolatry) without doing violence to the structure of the parable, what can they be? It makes most sense, I submit, to see them in terms of the "principles of religion" which Maimonides had taught in his juridical works, namely the "Thirteen Principles" of the *Commentary on the Mishnah* and the "Laws of the Foundations of the Torah" of the *Mishneh Torah*, texts addressed directly to the "jurists" of the fourth class.

Maimonides introduces his parable with the following words: "I shall begin the discourse in this chapter with a parable that I shall compose for you"[41] (p. 618). Now, while the *Guide* as a whole purports to be a private communication to Maimonides' disciple, Rabbi Joseph son of Rabbi Judah, there is no doubt that this claim is little more than a literary device.[42] Maimonides' opening words here seem, then, to be a signal that this text in particular is directly addressed to his disciple and individuals like him. This impression is strengthened by the marked emphasis on second person forms of address found in this chapter. This being the case, it seems to me folly to try to interpret the parable without knowing something of the qualifications of the reader to whom it is addressed. We cannot construct an intellectual portrait of the ideal reader of the *Guide*. We can, however, examine what is known about the individual disciple to whom the *Guide* was actually sent, and take him as an archetype of the ideal reader of the *Guide*. Three sources of information about Rabbi Joseph suggest themselves immediately: (a) what Maimonides says explicitly about him, (b) what Maimonides implies about him, and (c) what we know from other sources. All three agree that Rabbi Joseph was an accomplished Talmudic scholar. Maimonides tells us that the purpose of the *Guide* "is to give indications to a religious man for whom the validity of our Law has become established in his soul and has become actual in his belief—such a man being perfect in his religion and character. . . ." (I, Introduction, p. 5). He repeats much the same idea a bit further on: "My argument in the present Treatise is directed, as I have mentioned, to one who has philosophized and has knowledge of the true sciences but believes at the same time in the matters pertaining to the Law and is perplexed as to their meaning because of the uncertain terms and the parables" (p. 10). The student for whom Maimonides composed the *Guide*, therefore, is a committed Jew, learned in the sources of the tradition. This, of course, is also the impression gained from reading the *Guide*, replete as it is with literally thousands of biblical and rabbinic references. Maimonides assumes not only a high level of Jewish commitment on the part of his reader, but substantial rabbinic erudition as well. This meshes well with what we know about the actual career of Rabbi Joseph son of Rabbi Judah.[43] Having established, therefore, that the *Guide* in general and the parable of III 51 in particular are addressed to Talmudists, does it not make eminent sense to read the parable in those terms and understand the physicists of the fifth class who "have engaged in speculation concerning the fundamental principles of religion" to be scientifically trained Talmudists? This impression is strengthened even further when we recall Maimonides' words to his student (p. 619):

> Know, my son, that as long as you are engaged in studying the mathematical sciences and the art of logic, you are one of those who walk around the house searching for its gate. . . .If, however, you have understood the natural sciences, you have entered the habitation and are walking in the

antechambers. If, however, you have achieved perfection in the natural
sciences and have understood divine science, you have entered into the
ruler's place *into the inner court* and are with him in one habitation. This is
the rank of the men of science; they, however, are of different grades of
perfection.

Maimonides could not be clearer: when Rabbi Joseph ("my son") and
those like him, i.e., Talmudists, understand "the natural sciences," then
they have entered the habitation and become members of the fifth class.

Continuing with our interpretation of the parable, we return to the
next class, the sixth, comprised of individuals who "have entered the inner
court of the habitation and have come to be with the king, in one and the
same place with him, namely, in the ruler's habitation," without that
necessitating that they see the ruler or speak with him. People in this
class[44] have "achieved demonstration, to the extent that that is possible,
of everything that may be demonstrated," they have "ascertained in
metaphysics, to the extent that that is possible, everything that may be
ascertained," and they have "come close to certainty in those matters in
which one can only come close to it." In other words, they have achieved
philosophic perfection. These individuals "have achieved perfection in the
natural sciences," just like the individuals comprising the previous class,
but also "have understood divine science," that is, metaphysics, and have
achieved "the rank of the men of science."

Who are these indivduals? They are, I submit, a subset of those
Talmudists who make up the fifth class. In support of this claim, I note
that if my arguments with respect to the fifth class are convincing, then
they hold to a very great extent with respect to the members of the sixth
class as well, especially when we remember that Maimonides, in the text
cited just above from p. 619, describes the members of the sixth class as
being a subset of the members of the fifth class.

There is also a second argument which supports this contention. The
members of the sixth class, it will be recalled, have achieved perfection,
to one degree or another, in matters metaphysical. Let us look at the
prerequisites for achieving such perfection. One of the most important of
these is moral perfection. Maimonides is quite clear on the subject. In a
chapter (I 34) discussing impediments to the study of metaphysics,
Maimonides lists five such impediments. "The fourth," he writes, "is to
be found in the natural aptitudes. For it has been explained, in fact
demonstrated, that the moral virtues are a preparation for the rational
virtues, it being impossible to achieve true, rational acts −I mean perfect

rationality— unless it be by a man thoroughly trained in his morals and endowed with the qualities of tranquillity and quiet" (pp. 76-7). One cannot hope to achieve rational perfection, therefore, without having first achieved moral perfection.

We find this point reiterated in III 27 (p. 510). Maimonides informs us that "the Law as a whole is aimed at two things: the welfare of the soul and the welfare of the body." One of the ways in which the Law enhances the welfare of the body "consists in the acquisition by every human individual of moral qualities that are useful for life in society so that the affairs of the city may be ordered." This second aim, Maimonides then tells us, "is prior in nature and time," and "the first aim can only be achieved after achieving this second one." That intellectual perfection depends upon antecedent moral perfection is emphasized yet again in the last chapter of the Guide (III 54). Discussing the four types of perfection which pertain to human beings (possessions, constitution,[45] morals, and intellect), Maimonides says of the third:

> The third kind is a perfection that to a greater extent than the second kind subsists in the self. This is the perfection of the moral virtues. It consists in the individual's moral habits having attained their ultimate excellence. Most of the *commandments* serve no other end than the attainment of this kind of perfection. But this kind of perfection is likewise a preparation for something else and not an end in itself. . . . (p. 635)

Maimonides makes himself perfectly clear here. While moral perfection is surely to be valued above perfection of possessions and bodily constitution, it is not to be valued in and of itself, since it is a means to the attainment of a higher perfection. What is that higher perfection?

> The fourth kind is the true human perfection; it consists in the acquisition of the rational virtues—I refer to the conception of intelligibles, which teach true opinions concerning the divine things. This is in true reality the ultimate end; this is what gives the individual true perfection, a perfection belonging to him alone; and it gives him permanent perdurance; through it man is man. (p. 635)

While this text is important to us for many reasons, here I adduce it only in order to show how clearly Maimonides sees intellectual perfection as something which cannot be achieved without moral perfection. The latter is a "preparation" for the former.

We have shown that for Maimonides one must perfect one's morals to make possible the perfection of one's intellect.[46] Is moral perfection open to everyone? In theory, perhaps, it is. But in practice, it appears that Maimonides was extremely dubious about the possibility of a non-Jew achieving the sort of moral perfection necessary for intellectual perfection, at least in the pre-messianic world.

In *Guide* II 30 (p. 357), Maimonides cites with special emphasis the following dictum from the Talmud (Shabbat 146a):

> When the serpent came to Eve, it cast pollution into her. The pollution of [the sons of] Israel, who had been present at Mt. Sinai, has come to an end. [As for] the nations who were not present at Mt. Sinai, their pollution has not come to an end.

Maimonides' medieval and modern commentators are unanimous in reading this passage in the following fashion: man was subverted by his imagination and became subject to his physical appetites; the Jews, thanks to the Torah, are able to overcome their appetites and achieve moral and then intellectual perfection; not so the other nations of the world.[47]

That this is the purpose of the Torah is made clear in texts which we have lately adduced:

> The Law as a whole aims at two things: the welfare of the soul and the welfare of the body. . . .as for the welfare of the body, it comes about by the improvement of their ways of living one with another. This is achieved through two things. One of them is the abolition of their wronging each other. This is tantamount to every individual among the people not being permitted to act according to his will and up to the limits of his power, but being forced to do what is useful to the whole.

In other words, the Law comes to restrain us in the undisciplined exercise of our appetites.

The connection between the Torah and moral perfection is made explicitly in the text just cited, III 54 (p. 635): "Most of the *commandments* serve no other end than the attainment of this kind of perfection." Non-Jews, led by their imaginations and subjected to the tyranny of their appetites (thanks to the snake's "pollution"), and not having the Torah to perfect them, have little hope of ever achieving moral perfection. And if they have little hope of achieving moral perfection, then, as we have seen, they have precious little hope of achieving intellectual perfection.[48] This being so, it is hard to imagine that

Maimonides understood the members of the sixth class in the parable as anything but Talmudists who have gone on to study physics and then metaphysics.

But even individuals who have achieved this high status, despite their philosophic perfection, do not necessarily "see the ruler or speak to him." For that, it is necessary that "they should make another effort," and thus reach the seventh class. Having made that effort, "then they will be in the presence of the ruler." Those who have made this effort and reached the presence of the ruler are divided into four subclasses: (a) those who see the ruler from afar, (b) those who see the ruler from nearby, (c) those who hear the ruler's speech, and (d) those who speak with the ruler.

Of what does this additional effort consist? Maimonides explains:

> There are those who set their thought to work after having attained perfection in the divine science, turn wholly toward God, may He be cherished and held sublime, renounce what is other than He, and direct all the acts of their intellect toward an examination of beings with a view to drawing from them proof with regard to Him, so as to know His governance of them insofar as possible. These people are those present in the ruler's council. This is the rank of the prophets.

In other words, the members of this class —a subset of the previous class— have perfected themselves in metaphysics, but unlike the normal run of philosophers, these individuals go on to turn wholly toward God, renounce all other activities, and devote all their intellectual endeavors toward the examination of the world, not for its own sake, but in order to draw from it "proof with regard to Him." I suggest that this last be understood in the following fashion. Only two things exist: God and His creation. The signs of God in His creation are His attributes of action.[49] The "proof with regard to Him" which the perfected philosopher seeks has to do with the way in which God created, organized, and maintains the world. This understanding is confirmed by the next clause, which explains that the philosopher's examination is undertaken "so as to know His governance of them insofar as it is possible." Individuals, then, who perfect themselves as philosophers and then go on to devote themselves to God as just described are "present in the ruler's council" and achieve the rank of prophet. Prophets, then, are not simply "super philosophers" with highly developed imaginations, as they are often depicted as being.[50] Rather, they are individuals whose love of God dominates their entire lives.[51]

The seventh class of individuals described in the parable, then, are prophets. Prophets are a subset of philosophers. Philosophers are a subset of physicists. This being the case, and given that I adduced above convincing reasons for seeing the physicists in the parable as Jews, it follows that the seventh class in the parable consists of a small group of Jews. This, I suggest, both follows from and confirms my earlier interpretation: the third class consists of the Jewish masses; the fourth, Talmudists ("jurists"); the fifth, Talmudists who study physics; the sixth, Talmudists who study physics and metaphysics (like the ideal reader of the *Guide*); and the seventh, prophets, individuals who are expert in the Torah, who perfect themselves in the physical and metaphysical sciences, and who give themselves over wholly to God.

This interpretation is confirmed by the fact that while Maimonides very much wanted to preserve the *theoretical* possibility that non-Jews could prophesy (*contra* Halevi),[52] he sincerely thought that to all practical intents and purposes it was impossible that a non-Jew should reach the level of prophecy.[53] Moral perfection is one of the prerequisites of prophecy.[54] Since, as we have seen, moral perfection is next to impossible for non-Jews to attain, it follows that non-Jews cannot in this present world actually achieve the level of prophecy.

Thus Maimonides maintained that even Aristotle never achieved prophecy. In his well-known letter to Samuel ibn Tibbon, Maimonides says that there is no need to study the works of philosophers who preceded Aristotle because the works of Aristotle "are sufficient unto themselves [and encompass] everything that was composed before them. His intellect,[55] Aristotle's, is the extreme limit of human intellect, apart from him upon whom the divine emanation has flowed forth to such an extent that they[56] reach the level of prophecy, there being no level higher."[57] So Aristotle achieved the pinnacle of intellectual perfection available to humans who do not reach prophecy, but went no higher. If Aristotle could not make the breakthrough from intellectual perfection to prophecy, can we seriously entertain the idea that Maimonides held that other gentiles could?

Maimonides concludes his explanation of the parable with a few lines about the special character of Mosaic prophecy, the highest level of attainment ever reached by a human being.[58]

The explication of the parable offered here leads to the conclusion that Maimonides' description of the various levels of perfection open to Jews —obedience to the Law, juridical competence, expertise in the principles of religion and physics, expertise in metaphysics, prophecy, and Mosaic prophecy— is strictly hierarchical and ever narrowing: each class is a subset of the one before it, maintains the perfection of the class before it, and adds its own particular perfection. Prophets are Jews who obey the commandments, achieve expertise in halakhah, study the principles of religion and physics, achieve perfection in metaphysics, and give themselves over wholly to the worship of God. These facts will be important when we come to analyze the end of III 54, where the perfected individual is called upon to dedicate his or her life to loving-kindness, righteousness, and judgment.

Having concluded his exposition of the parable, Maimonides reverts

> to the subject of this chapter, which is to confirm men in the intention to set
> their thought to work on God alone after they have achieved knowledge of
> Him, as we have explained. This is the worship peculiar to those who have
> apprehended the true realities; the more they think of Him and of being with
> Him, the more their worship increases. (p. 620)

Here at the end of the entire argument, these words seem clearly to state that the intention of III 51 is to take individuals who have achieved the sort of knowledge of God which Maimonides has described, i.e., individuals who have achieved perfection in metaphysics, and encourage them "to set their thought to work on God alone." Those who have perfected themselves in metaphysics, we have seen, and succeed in turning "wholly toward God" are the prophets. Their activity is called "worship." Summarizing the exegesis of Maimonides offered to this point once more, we may say that prophets are philosophically erudite Talmudists who turn from all activities but the contemplation of God's works.[59]

Maimonides now contrasts the worship just described with that of the individual without philosophical attainments. Such a one does not truly worship God, but a non-existent, imaginary being.[60] The true worshipper seeks always to strengthen the bond between God and himself or herself, this bond being the intellect (p. 620). From this we learn that even the person who has achieved intellectual perfection and turns toward God exclusively cannot "rest on his or her laurels," so to speak, but must constantly cultivate the intellectual bond. Intellectual perfection is not like money in the bank. Like health or vigor, it takes hard work to keep it "fresh."[61] Once we apprehend God, Maimonides informs us (p. 621), we love Him: "love is proportionate to apprehension." As a result of loving God, we can worship Him. We have, then, the progression:

knowledge, love, worship. Love is more than simply additional knowledge, just as the worship described above is more than love. The prophet, then, the true worshipper of God, is much more than a philosopher with a healthy imagination. Maimonides concludes this passage by noting, "mostly this [prophetic worship] is achieved in solitude and isolation. Hence every excellent man stays frequently in solitude and does not meet anyone unless it is necessary."[62] It is not clear whether or not Maimonides wanted to make prophets of all those who reached the highest stage or only true worshippers.

Maimonides reaffirms the importance of maintaining the intellectual bond between man and God (pp. 621-2) and gives practical advice on how to achieve intellectual worship (pp. 622-623). He then explains the special character of the worship of Moses and the Patriarchs. An individual of this class "achieves a state in which he talks with people and is occupied with his bodily necessities while His intellect is wholly turned toward Him, may He be exalted, so that in His heart he is always in His presence, may He be exalted, while outwardly he is with people. . . ." (p. 623). Abraham, Isaac, Jacob, and Moses, then, reached a state wherein they could continue their regular activities while inwardly retaining the solitude necessary for the highest level of communion with God. Moreover, these men were so clearly linked with God that He became known to the world through them, His name linked with theirs (p. 624).

After mentioning the special providence extended to individuals like Moses and the Patriarchs, Maimonides points out that even in their everyday actions, "their end was to come near to Him" (p. 624):[63] "the end of their efforts during their life was to bring into being a religious community that would know and worship God. . . . to spread the doctrine of *the unity of the Name in the world* and to guide people to love Him. . . ." The Patriarchs and Moses, then, sought to teach the doctrine of one God and bring people to love and worship Him. Since, as Maimonides never tires of informing us, the "intent of the whole Law and the pole around which it revolves is to put an end to idolatry,"[64] the perfection of the Patriarchs and Moses found expression in their attempts to bring people closer to God. Here we have the highest level of contemplation, which finds its expression in the action of bringing other people closer to the God.[65]

Maimonides then involves himself in a lengthy discussion of the special providence vouchsafed to prophets and other perfected individuals, disingenuously introducing it, however, as "a most extraordinary speculation" which just occurred to him at that moment in the writing of the chapter.[66] I have no idea why he did this.

He closes the chapter with a discussion of the special nature of the death of the true worshipper, which is actually a kind of release.[67] Maimonides concludes with the words,

> Bring your soul to understand this chapter, and direct your efforts to the multiplying of those times in which you are with God or endeavoring to approach Him and to decreasing those times in which you are with other than Him and in which you make no efforts to approach Him. This guidance is sufficient in view of the purpose of this Treatise. (p. 628)

This concluding exhortation makes clear a point to which we alluded above and explains, it seems, how Maimonides could call both for solitude and for work in bringing other people closer to Torah: the reader is called upon to decrease those times in which he or she is neither involved with God nor trying to approach Him. In other words, we are called upon to seek to increase our nearness to God while at the same time continuing in our efforts to bring others closer to Torah. Thus, Maimonides calls upon us to emulate Moses and the Patriarchs, pursuing inward solitude while at the same time following our daily activities. This is not a goal which we can actually reach. Speaking of the rank of Moses and the Patriarchs, Maimonides said (p. 624): "This rank is not a rank that, with a view to the attainment of which, someone like myself may aspire for guidance."[68] Maimonides, then, concludes this chapter (III 51) by setting up an ideal toward which we should aspire, even if we cannot realize it fully in our lives.

Chapter III 52 is a short chapter, but one which raises some interesting problems.[69] For our purposes, however, it will suffice to note that a person who chooses the path of human perfection must know that he or she is constantly being examined by God. Such knowledge stimulates awe and fear of God. It is the purpose of the actions commanded by the Torah to bring us to this awe and fear. This shows the importance of the commandments of the Torah for the achieving of human perfection. The doctrines taught by the Torah, on the other hand, teach us the love of God. Maimonides cites as examples of the doctrines taught by the Torah which bring us to the love of God "the apprehension of His being as He is in truth, may He be exalted" and "His unity" (p. 629).

The doctrinal teachings of the Torah, therefore, would appear to be superior to the actional commandments, since service of God out of love is superior to service of God out of fear.[70] This would seem to support those who interpret Maimonides as teaching that ultimate perfection is intellectual. This conclusion, however, must be modified by the fact that for Maimonides love of God finds expression in the fulfillment of His commands. Abraham, we are told (III 24, pp. 500-1) was willing to sacrifice Isaac not only because of his fear of God, but also "because of his love to carry out His command."[71] The performance of the commandments should be seen as a means toward achieving the end of acceptance of the doctrinal teachings of the Torah; this acceptance is, in turn, as will be made clear below, a means toward the proper performance of the commandments, as in the case of Abraham.

Chapter III 53 is given over to a discussion of the terms loving-kindness, judgment, and righteousness. In addition to defining the terms (so that they can be used, Maimonides informs us, in the following chapter), Maimonides points out (p. 632) that these terms, when applied to God, refer to His actions. His loving-kindness finds expression in the creation of the world; His righteousness, "in the providence over living beings through their own natural powers"; and His judgment, "in the occurrence of the world of relative good things and relative great calamities, necessitated by judgment that is consequent upon wisdom." This text seems open to two radically different interpretations: God's loving-kindness, judgment, and righteousness find expression in His creation, providence, and judging of the world, or they find expression exclusively through the forces of nature working in the world. The latter is consistent with the naturalist interpretation of Maimonides proposed by Berman and Pines. I will indicate below why I find this interpretation unconvincing.

We may now turn to chapter III 54. Maimonides opens the chapter with a discussion of the term "wisdom." In Maimonides' analysis, "the term *wise* can be applied to one possessing the rational virtues, to one possessing the moral virtues, to everyone skilled in a practical art, and to one who uses ruses in working evil and wickedness" (p. 633). The wisdom of him "who knows the whole of the Law in its true reality," however, is defined in terms of "the rational virtues comprised in the Law and in respect of the moral virtues included in it."

The rational content of the Torah has been transmitted from generation to generation through tradition without its attendant proofs.[72]

For this reason, people came mistakenly to distinguish between philosophy and the Torah. Philosophy was thought to provide the proof of the rational matter transmitted   by tradition. It is in this sense, Maimonides explains, that the Sages distinguish between Torah and wisdom. The Torah, in this dichotomy, teaches the results of philosophical speculation (first and foremost, the doctrines of God's existence, unity, and incorporeality), while philosophy provides the rational proofs. Maimonides summarizes the view of the Sages on the proper relationship between these things as follows:

> . . . .man is required first to obtain knowledge of the Torah, then to obtain wisdom, then to know what is incumbent upon him with regard to the legal science of the Law[73] —that is, the drawing of inferences concerning what one ought to do. And this should be the order observed: The opinions in question should first be known as   received through tradition; then they should be demonstrated; then the actions through which one's way of life may be ennobled should be precisely defined. (pp. 633-4)

At first reading, it might be thought that Maimonides is suggesting that one achieve a high level of philosophical perfection (the ability to demonstrate the truth of the correct opinions taught by the Torah) before beginning to define halakhah. That is, of course, absurd. Obedience to the dictates of the law is the basic duty of all Jews, the simple and those destined for philosophical perfection alike. The sequence of behavior described here relates to the obligations of those who seek perfection. Maimonides, as Twersky has shown,[74] teaches that halakhic obedience is a prerequisite for intellectual perfection, while that perfection itself brings us to a higher level of halakhic obedience, one which ennobles our lives.[75] It ennobles our lives, I suggest, because this sort of halakhic obedience is not performed in order to earn a reward (since the intellectually perfected know that there is no "tit for tat" reward for the observance of the commandments, contrary to what the vulgar believe). They act purely out of love of God and a desire to imitate Him.

Maimonides then describes the four perfections which "ancient and modern philosophers" have said may be found in human beings.[76] These, as we noted above, are wealth, temperament, morals, and intellect. We quoted above texts from this discussion which seem to show Maimonides valuing intellectual perfection above all others. Maimonides supports his analysis through an exegesis of Jeremiah 9:22-23, asserting that the prophet and the Sages agree that wisdom, meaning the apprehension of

God, is the end toward which all the other perfections (including obedience to the commandments) are but preparations.

But Maimonides concludes the chapter and the book with a passage which seems to contradict what he has just said. The point of the prophet here in the verses under discussion is to explain humankind's "noblest ends." The prophet, however, "does not limit them only to the apprehension of Him, may He be exalted." Rather, Jeremiah says "that one should glory in the apprehension of Myself and in the knowledge of My attributes, by which he means His actions" (p. 637). Maimonides goes on to explain that knowledge of God's attributes means knowledge of God's actions and says that he made this clear in his exposition of the verse, *Show me now Thy ways.* . . . (Ex. 33:13). The only other place in all his writings where Maimonides cites this verse is in *Guide* I 54.[77] Maimonides summarizes his discussion of God's attributes of action there (a discussion which has an extremely naturalistic tone) in the words, "we have made clear why Scripture, in enumerating His actions, has confined itself here to those mentioned above, and that those actions are needed for the governance of cities" (pp. 127-8).

Why has Scripture confined itself here, in this particular context (Exodus 33:13), to actions needed for the governance of cities? The answer to this question may be found if we examine the context of the verse:

> The Lord spoke unto Moses: "Depart, go up hence, thou and the people that thou hast brought up out of the land of Egypt. . . ." (Ex. 33:1). . .And the Lord said unto Moses: "Say unto the children of Israel: 'Ye are a stiff-necked people. . . .,'" (33:5). . .And Moses said unto the Lord: "See Thou sayest unto me: 'Bring up this people'; and Thou hast not let me know whom Thou wilt send with me. Yet Thou hast said, 'I know thee by name, and thou hast also found grace in my sight'. Now, therefore, I pray Thee, if I have found grace in Thy sight, show me now Thy ways, that I may know Thee, to the end that I may find grace in Thy sight and consider that this nation is Thy people." (33:12-13)

The context determined by these verses, then, is Moses' need to govern God's people and the difficulties he encountered in doing so. It was the need to govern the Jews that was Moses' "ultimate object in his demand, the conclusion of what he says being: *that I may know Thee, to the end that I may find grace in Thy sight and consider that this nation is Thy people*—that is, a people for the government of whom I need to perform actions that I must seek to make similar to Thy actions in governing them" (p. 125).

In I 54, Maimonides teaches that we ought to imitate God's attributes and that the attributes which ought to be imitated are the attributes of action. But which of God's attributes of action ought to be imitated? For Moses, the answer is given in Exodus 33, as interpreted by Maimonides in I 54. For everyone else, that is to say, for everyone else who achieves the high level of intellectual perfection which makes possible imitation of God, the answer is given in Jeremiah 9:23, as interpreted by Maimonides in III 54. Jeremiah "makes it clear to us that those actions that ought to be known and imitated are *loving-kindness, judgment,* and *righteousness"* (p. 637).

Maimonides sums up in the last sentences of the book proper:

> It is clear that the perfection of man that may truly be gloried in is the one acquired by him who has achieved, in a measure corresponding to his capacity, apprehension of Him, may He be exalted, and who knows His providence extending over His creatures as manifested in the act of bringing them into being and in their governance as it is. The way of life of such an individual, after he has achieved this apprehension, will always have in view *loving-kindness, righteousness,* and *judgment,* through emulation of His actions, may He be exalted, as we have explained several times in this Treatise.

In this passage we discover that beyond intellectual perfection there is an additional perfection, the one "that may truly be gloried in." This is the perfection of the individual who not only apprehends God to the greatest extent possible for him or her (straightforward philosophical perfection) but also understands God's providence as expressed in creation and God's governance of His creatures. A person who has achieved this level of understanding will always seek to practice loving-kindness, righteousness, and judgment, thereby imitating God.

Important keys for understanding this passage are the terms "creation" and "providence." If one understands Maimonides as ultimately denying that God created the world by an act of will and further understands Maimonides as affirming providence only in what Maimonides himself calls the Aristotelian sense of the term, namely, that providence means the uninterrupted workings of the laws of nature,[78] then one will be led to interpret this passage, as do Berman and Pines, in light of I 54 and in a very naturalistic way. Such an interpretation leaves little room for *imitatio Dei* in any but political terms. If, however, one affirms, as I do, that Maimonides held that God created the world by will and further affirms that God extends His providence to humans on the basis of their intellectual attainments, then one can hardly read this passage in the way Berman and Pines do. This is not an issue which can be settled clearly through textual or historical argument. Maimonides left too many red herrings on his trail to make that possible. The most that can be done is to present a reading of Maimonides that does as little violence as possible to the man and to his writings, makes as much sense as possible, and raises the fewest possible problems. That is what I have been trying to do to this point and what I shall continue to do here.

One of the central problems raised by this text from the end of the *Guide* is the issue of the relationship between intellectual perfection and action and the related issue of the apparent tension between Maimonides' intellectualist account of human perfection at the beginning of the *Guide* and his demand here for *imitatio Dei* as an outcome of intellectual perfection. I propose to deal with these issues below. There are other issues which must be discussed first, including Maimonides' conception of the imitation of God. Before turning to that, however, I think that it will be helpful to summarize, if only in the briefest way, the exegesis of III 51-54 offered to this point.

All four chapters subserve a practical end: to bring certain individuals to devote themselves entirely to God after they have achieved knowledge of Him. This appears to be the point of the *Guide of the Perplexed* as a whole. It is important to note that Maimonides' intent seems to be that each individual (among those who are capable of perfection) should, after achieving the level of intellectual perfection possible for him or her, then turn to devotion to God. This seems to be the point of the concrete advice for achieving this aim which Maimonides gives his readers in III 51. It is also important to note that this single-minded devotion to God alone is not inconsistent with life in the world, even though we cannot actually hope to achieve the level of the Patriarchs in this regard.

In the parable of the palace, we learn that prophecy presupposes intellectual perfection, which in turn presupposes halakhic perfection. Prophets, we have seen, are philosophically erudite Talmudists who turn inwardly from all activities but the contemplation of God's works. The Patriarchs, pre-eminent prophets, managed to preserve this inward devotion while engaging in practical activity. The nature of that activity was to bring people closer to the Torah. Their imitation of God, then, should be seen in primarily halakhic terms. This is not to deny that such imitation has a political aspect. Both Abraham and Moses in effect founded political communities, engaged in warfare, entered into negotiations with foreign potentates, and enforced law. But to see their imitation of God primarily in these terms is, as I have been at pains to show, a misrepresentation of Maimonides, if not necessarily of Al-Farabi. Let me be as clear as I can: there surely is a political component in the imitation of God after the achievement of intellectual perfection, as the example of Moses and the Patriarchs proves. But that political element ought not to be exaggerated, or be presented in purely naturalist or what we today would call secularist terms. The political life is not the best life; rather, the best life has a political dimension.

Obedience to the laws of the Torah is both a condition for achieving true intellectual perfection (in most, but not all cases: witness Aristotle) and a consequence of it. There is, then, as Berman himself notes, an imitation of God before intellectual perfection and an imitation of God after such perfection.[79] Put in other words, we obey God before intellectual perfection out of fear and after intellectual perfection out of love.

Chapter Four

Imitatio Dei

Berman and Pines interpret the last passage of chapter III 54 in the light of I 54 and conclude that loving-kindness, righteousness, and judgment refer to the sort of political leadership discussed in that earlier chapter. They ignore the way in which Maimonides indicates that his focus in I 54 is determined by the verses he is explicating there. Cohen, Guttmann, and Schwarzschild interpret this passage in the light of Kant's moral philosophy and insist that loving-kindness, righteousness and judgment refer to ordinary moral qualities. They ignore the fact that Maimonides explicitly rejects moral virtue as an ultimate goal and use, as I will indicate below, a vocabulary totally inappropriate to Maimonides' thought.

The correct way to interpret this passage, I submit, is in light of Maimonides' biography as a whole, in light of the *Guide* as a whole, and in light of the four chapters which form the immediate context of the passage. These chapters are, of course, III 51-54. Reading these chapters as I have done in this essay, we are ineluctably led to the conclusion that the way in which we imitate God through the practice of loving-kindness, righteousness, and judgment is through the fulfillment of the commandments of the Torah after having achieved as high a level of intellectual perfection as is possible for us.

In order to see this, it will be helpful to discuss the notion of the imitation of God as it reached Maimonides and particularly as he interpreted it. Maimonides was heir to two different traditions concerning *imitatio Dei*, one based upon the classic sources of Greek thought and its Islamic interpreters and one based on Biblical and rabbinic texts. The first of these traditions opened with a famous statement of Plato's:

> Socrates: Evils, Theodorus, can never pass away; for there must always remain something which is antagonistic to good. Having no place among the gods in heaven, of necessity they hover around the mortal nature, and this earthly sphere. Wherefore we ought to fly away from earth to heaven as quickly as we can; and to fly away *is to become like God, as far as this is possible*: and to become like him, is to become holy, just, and wise.[1]

41

Lawrence V. Berman has followed the history of this conception of the imitation of God in medieval philosophic texts.[2] Despite their many differences, and despite the fact that many, like those by Plato, make some reference to the practical consequences of *imitatio Dei*, the fact still remains that the overwhelming emphasis in all these texts is on imitating God by becoming like Him. This should hardly surprise us, given the Platonizing tendency of ancient philosophy to ontologize everything.[3]

The Jewish tradition of *imitatio Dei* took a different course. It finds its earliest expression, of course, in the Torah, with verses such as the following: *Ye shall be holy, for I the Lord your God am holy* (Lev. 19:2); *And now, Israel, what doth the Lord thy God require of thee, but to fear the Lord thy God, to walk in all His ways, and to love Him, and to serve the Lord thy God with all thy heart and with all thy soul* (Deut. 10:12); and *The Lord will establish thee for a holy people unto Himself, as He hath sworn unto thee; if thou shalt keep the commandments of the Lord thy God, and walk in His ways* (Deut. 28:9). Despite the fact that the first of these three verses could have been used to justify the form of *imitatio Dei* found in philosophic texts (in the sense of becoming like God), the post-Biblical texts developed an idea of *imitatio Dei* which involved, not *becoming* like God, but *acting* like God. The specification of these ways, as should be clear from the two verses from Deuteronomy just cited, is the halakhah ("the way"), the commandments of the Torah.[4]

How did Maimonides treat this issue? He deals explicitly with the imitation of God in three works: the *Book of Commandments*, the *Mishneh Torah*, and the *Guide of the Perplexed*. The eighth positive commandment in the first of these works reads as follows:

> Walking in God's ways: By this injunction we are commanded to be like God (praised be He) as far as it is in our power. This injunction is contained in His words, *and walk in His ways* [Deut. 28:9], and also in an earlier verse in His words [*What doth the Lord thy God require of thee, but to fear the Lord thy God,*] *to walk in all His ways* [Deut. 10:12]. On this latter verse the Sages comment as follows: "Just as the Holy One, blessed be He, is called Merciful, so shouldst thou be merciful; just as He is called Gracious, so shouldst thou be gracious; just as He is called Righteous, so shouldst thou be righteous; just as He is called Saintly [*hasid*], so shouldst thou be saintly.[5] This injunction has already appeared in another form, in His words, *After the Lord shall ye walk* [Deut. 13:5], which the Sages explain as meaning that we are to imitate the acts of lovingkindness and sublime attributes by which the Lord (exalted be He) is described in a figurative way—for He is immeasurably exalted above all such description.[6]

Maimonides counts as a commandment, then, the obligation to become like God.[7] He explains that one fulfills this commandment, not by turning oneself into a being similar to God,[8] but by imitating certain[9] of God's attributes of action.

Maimonides codifies *imitatio Dei* as a law once again in the *Mishneh Torah*. In the list of commandments preceding the work, he counts as a commandment, "to imitate His ways, as it says, *And walk in His ways*" [Deut. 28:9]. This commandment is explicated in "Laws of Moral Qualities," where it is introduced at the beginning of the section once again as a commandment "to imitate His ways." The first five chapters of this work are given over to specifying the detailed requirements of this commandment, without, however, being explicitly described as such. The issue is taken up directly in only one paragraph (I 6):

> We are bidden to walk in the middle paths which are the right and proper ways, as it is said, *And walk in His ways*. In explanation of the text just quoted the Sages taught: "Even as God is called gracious, be thou gracious; even as He is called merciful, be thou merciful; even as He is called holy, be thou holy." Thus, too, the prophets described the Almighty by all the various attributes, "long-suffering, abounding in kindness, righteous and upright, perfect, mighty and powerful," and so forth to teach us that these qualities are good and right and that a human being should cultivate them, and thus imitate God, as far as he can.[10]

In contrast to the *Book of Commandments*, where Maimonides first codifies the law as calling on Jews to become like God and then explains that in terms of imitating certain of God's attributes of action, here in the *Mishneh Torah*, in all three places where Maimonides explicitly mentions this law, it is described only in terms of imitating God's actions.

Given Maimonides' teachings on the unknowability of God, it should not surprise us that in the *Guide* this emphasis on the imitation of God's actions and not of God Himself finds clear expression. At the end of I 54 (p. 128), Maimonides writes:

> For the utmost virtue of man is to become like unto Him, may He be exalted, as far as he is able; which means that we should make our actions like unto His, as the Sages made clear when interpreting the verse, *Ye shall be holy* (Lev. 19:2). They said, *He is gracious, so be you also gracious; He is merciful, so be you also merciful.*

This text has some interesting points about it. Perhaps the most interesting is that the statement from the Sages which Maimonides quoted by way of explaining Leviticus 19:2 is not a comment on that verse at all. Maimonides himself connects a fuller version of it to Deuteronomy 28:9 in "Laws of Moral Qualities," I 6, as we have just seen. A slightly different version of the passage is connected to Deuteronomy 10:12 in *Book of Commandments*. In no source which I have been able to locate is the passage, in any of its forms, presented as a commentary on Leviticus 19:2.[11]

I suggest that Maimonides' behavior here can be explained as follows. The verse, *Ye shall be holy for I the Lord thy God am holy*, is the one traditionally cited in support of the philosophic view of *imitatio Dei*. To emphasize the Jewish approach, imitation of God's ways, in his halakhic works Maimonides ignores this verse altogether. In his more clearly philosophic work, however, directed to individuals familiar to one degree or another with the philosophic literature, Maimonides may have felt it wise to draw the sting implicit in this verse by citing it in the context of *imitatio Dei* and explaining it —with the added authority of the Sages— in the light of the Jewish approach.

Maimonides cites this verse in two other places. In the fourth of the fourteen principles with which he introduces his *Book of Commandments*, he interprets it as a commandment to fulfill all the commandments of the Torah.[12] He quotes the verse again in the *Guide*, in III 47 (p. 595), quoting the *Sifra* to the effect that this verse "concerns sanctification by the commandments." Wherever Maimonides cites this verse, then, he gives it an unequivocally practical interpretation.

Maimonides makes implicit use of the issue of *imitatio Dei* in our text from the end of III 54.[13] There human perfection is seen in terms of the practice of loving-kindness, righteousness, and judgment. Of what does this practice consist? How does one imitate God after intellectual perfection has been achieved? Is it through politics of a special sort, through morality, or through obedience to the commandments? I submit that the last answer is correct.

It would be easy to prove the point on the basis of Maimonides' halakhic texts, since they elucidate verses which make the point explicitly.[14] But support for this interpretation can be found in the *Guide* itself. For Maimonides cites Leviticus 19:2 (*Ye shall be holy for I the Lord thy God am holy*) as the source for the obligation to imitate God. This is the only verse cited explicitly in support of this obligation in the *Guide*. And it is this verse, as we have seen, which Maimonides explains, in the only other place it appears in the *Guide*, as concerning "sanctification by the commandments." One imitates God, therefore, by fulfilling His commandments. The care with which Maimonides chose his words and texts is well known.[15] It seems unlikely that it is a coincidence that Maimonides chose as his only proof-text for the obligation to imitate God a verse which he himself explains, in the only two other places where he cites it (in the *Guide* and in the *Book of Commandments*), as meaning the fulfillment of the commandments. It is almost as if he told us explicitly: "The obligation to imitate God, even when expressed in a verse which might be construed as expressing the philosophical conception of *imitatio Dei*, is fulfilled through obedience to the commandments of the Torah."

Chapter Five

Critique of the Moral and Political Interpretations of Perfection

Up to this point I have been concerned with showing how a correct reading of the last four chapters of the *Guide* leads to two conclusions: (a) the purely intellectualist interpretation of human perfection in Maimonides is incorrect; and (b) Maimonides actually held that *after* one achieves intellectual perfection, one is called upon to imitate God through the fulfillment of the commandments of the Torah. The proponents of what I have been calling the moral and political interpretations of Maimonides agree with the first point and part of the second. We all agree that the intellectually perfected is called upon to imitate God. Cohen, Guttmann, and Schwarzschild maintain, however, that that imitation is expressed through moral behavior; Strauss, Berman, and Pines maintain that that imitation is expressed through statesmanship; Twersky and Hartman maintain that that imitation is expressed through fulfillment of the commandments of the Torah. I agree with that interpretation, with the added proviso that the fulfillment of the commandments of the Torah has an undeniably political aspect. The interpretation of Maimonides which I propose here may be strengthened if I explain why, despite our many areas of agreement, I still reject the first two alternative approaches.

Steven Schwarzschild has given the fullest and most detailed defense of the moral interpretation of human perfection in his "Moral Radicalism and 'Middlingness' in the Ethics of Maimonides."[1] There is much more in this brilliant and erudite essay with which I agree than with which I disagree. In fact, the disagreement between us may turn out to be purely semantic since Schwarzschild himself indicates that the morality he is concerned to prove lies at the basis of Maimonides' conception of *imitatio Dei* is "embodied in Jewish law" (p. 75). But even if that is the case, I think that in interpreting a text one ought to use to the greatest extent possible terminology which reflects the orientation of the author of the text, and one certainly ought not to use terminology which the author of the text would consciously reject.[2] Thus, even if Schwarzschild means by morality nothing more than a perfectionist approach to the primacy of the practical life (expressed as such, I have no quarrel with him), he ought not to call it "morality" if he claims to be explicating Maimonides.

Substantively, there are difficulties with the way in which Schwarzschild works out his argument. He summarizes "the lengthy and complex arguments of the *Guide*" in the following fashion:

> Man's purpose in life is to unite to the greatest possible degree with the deity (through the "conjunction" of his "acquired intellect" with the Active Intellect). The deity, now, is exhaustively described by the totality of his "negative" and actional attributes. The negative attributes have the effect of emptying the universe of God —that is, nothing in or about the universe is in any manner comparable and, therefore, even the less identifiable with God; the universe, and man as part of it, are completely "secular." Thus, an infinite gap is opened between God and the world. This gap is bridged only by His attributes of action— descriptions of what God does in relationship to the world, not of what he is (in himself). These attributes of action furthermore possess two features which must be particularly noted: 1) no inference may be drawn from what God does to what he is (so that, for example, he loves, but he is not a lover), and connected therewith, 2) the attributes of action are legitimately imputable to the deity only because and to the extent to which they serve as models which are to be imitated by man in his moral life (pp. 69-70).

If "no inference can be drawn from what God does to what he is," how can Schwarzschild tell us on the very next page, "there is then no God but the moral imperative"? By calling God "the moral imperative," Schwarzschild is not simply saying that God is the sum total of His moral actions. Such a move might be thought to save him from the criticism that he is illegitimately positively describing God. He needs the claim "'God' = morality" (i.e., that the referent of the word 'God' is the same as the referent of the word 'morality') in order to prove that Maimonides' conception of intellectual perfection is at basis moral.[3] Such a move, furthermore, leaves him open to the criticisms which Pines levelled against Cohen and Guttmann (and which Schwarzschild does not, I submit, succeed in rebutting), namely, that many of God's actions described in the *Guide* cannot, by any stretch of the imagination, be made to fit our ordinary conceptions of morality.[4] This brings us to a second problem. Schwarzschild's claim that "the attributes of action are legitimately imputable to the deity only because and to the extent to which they serve as models which are to be imitated by man in his moral life" is, I think, simply wrong.[5] Does Schwarzschild mean to include among the attributes of action which we are to imitate creation, wily deceit, vengeance, and the wholesale destruction of populations?[6] We cannot create worlds, and it is doubtful if Schwarzschild would want us to imitate God by practicing deceit, vengeance, and wholesale destruction.

In sum, I think Schwarzschild is guilty of exactly what he condemns Strauss for: "the stubborn insistence on reading his own theologico-political ideology into the classical texts" (p. 81). The ideology which Schwarzschild stubbornly reads into Maimonides has the advantage of being essentially translatable into Maimonidean terms. In this, his position is surely superior to that of Strauss, Pines, and Berman. I should now like to show why this is so.

Berman has given the fullest exposition of the political interpretation of human perfection in Maimonides. His exposition is connected to, and depends upon, two methodological assumptions, both of which I reject. First, Berman, like Pines, reads Maimonides in basically naturalistic terms, as a philosopher who, for a variety of reasons, pretends to be a rabbi.[7] Second (and I hope that I am not being unfair here), Berman seems to me to use *quellensforschung* in an exaggerated fashion. Wolfson says of Spinoza, "if we could cut up all the philosophic literature available to him into slips of paper, toss them up into the air, and let them fall back on the ground, then out of these scattered slips of paper we could reconstruct his *Ethics*."[8] Berman appears to approach Maimonides in like fashion, reading him as little more than "the disciple of Al-Farabi." Thus he writes:

> The point of my title ["Maimonides, the Disciple of Alfarabi"] is that Maimonides was also the disciple of Alfarabi in the area of the relationship between religion, jurisprudence, theology, and philosophy. I should like to argue as well and in conformity with the preceding that Maimonides did what no one else did explicitly in medieval Middle Eastern culture. He took the Alfarabian theory of the relationship between philosophy, religion, jurisprudence and theology and applied it in a thorough-going manner to a particular religion, Judaism. His approach takes on new significance and greater clarity once we have put on our Alfarabian spectacles. Doubtless, there were many intellectuals who accepted the Alfarabian view and tried to understand Judaism and Christianity from its perspective, but no one else in a major work attempted to apply his theory in detail to a particular religious tradition.[9]

This approach ignores Maimonides' biography, his personal religious commitments as expressed in his life and writings, and the community to which he insisted on attaching himself. Berman further seems to ignore the fact that Al-Farabi was, at least, nominally, a Muslim writing for other

Muslims while Maimonides was, at least nominally (and, I think, much more than nominally), a Jew writing for other Jews. Approaching Maimonides in this fashion has the further disadvantage of ignoring his creativity and treating him as a thinker content to do little more than transpose Al-Farabi into a Jewish idiom.[10] None of this is to imply that Maimonides was not influenced by Al-Farabi. The question is not whether or not Maimonides read and was influenced by Al-Farabi to one extent or another, but whether or not he may fairly be characterized as an "Al-Farabian" with respect to the question of human perfection.

Berman's most recent statement of his thesis is found in his "Maimonides on Political Leadership."[11] He first makes the wholly unobjectionable claim that "action in imitation of God after intellectual perfection is on a higher plane than practical activity before achieving theoretical perfection" (p. 116). It is in spelling out the sort of imitation envisioned that we part company. The relationship of the philosopher to the state, according to Berman, is the same as that of God to the universe: "the philosopher needs, after intellectual perception, to imitate God by means of his desire to found a more perfect society. Just as God acts in the realm of nature so the philosopher acts in the realm of voluntary things and it is his duty to *found* an ideal state and preserve it."[12] This position reflects Al-Farabi's claim that the "meaning of the Imam, of the philosopher, and of the law-giver is identical." About this he writes:

> It is thus necessary that a law-giver, whose essence is that of a Ruler, not of a servant, be a philosopher, and, conversely, in the case of the philosopher who has acquired theoretical virtues, these acquisitions would be worthless if he does not possess the ability to realize them in all other people in so far as this is possible. . . .Thus the meaning of the Imam, of the philosopher, and of the lawgiver is identical.[13]

The ideal individual, therefore, the only truly perfected philosopher, must, by his or her very nature, also be the prophetic king who founds a new society (Al-Farabi's "Virtuous City"[14]) by legislating its laws.

This perception makes sense in an Islamic context. State and religion are intimately connected in Islam,[15] Muslim philosophers could and did play political roles,[16] and Islam was indeed created by a prophet who founded a new society and whose followers, no doubt, were sure that if philosophy was a perfection, then he was philosophically perfected. Indeed, as Fazlur Rahman notes, "the philosophers themselves categorically deny that any and every thinker or mystic could be a prophet and indeed as our anlysis showed, *they had in their mind certain fixed images, of Muhammad par excellence.*"[17]

This doesn't make   sense in a Jewish context. Since the fall of Jerusalem, Jews had renounced temporal power and involvement[18] and were well aware of the fact that political activity and statesmanship were not open to them.[19] The view of Al-Farabi makes excellent sense in a context where the legislative prophet was the last prophet ("the seal of the prophets"). He can allow himself, therefore, to maintain that the true sign of the prophet is that he founds a state. If we translate that into Jewish terms, however, we must say that Moses was the only true prophet. What are we to do with all the other prophets, both the Patriarchs who preceded Moses and the prophets who followed him? We could, of course, argue that by "prophet" *per se*, Maimonides means only Moses, and call all the other so-called prophets by some other term. But that, unfortunately, is not what Maimonides says. He does, of course, distinguish Moses from all the other prophets but maintains that the others are prophets while Moses is something more.[20] Further, we have no evidence that Maimonides was willing to maintain that Moses was the only true philosopher, thus excluding Aristotle, for example, from that category.

Furthermore, in Berman's view we are called upon to imitate God in ways which are only suitable for Moses (i.e., through legislation by which we found an ideal society) and in ways which are wholly unconnected with our previous training (which, as we have seen above, has been limited to Talmudics, the propaedeutic sciences, physics, and metaphysics[21]). In the view which I have been urging here, on the other hand, we are called upon to imitate God by following *in His ways*, as we have been trained to do throughout our lives, through obedience to his commandments. This does not exclude the political virtues, of course, but nor do they exhaust the realm of the imitation of God.

Actually, in Berman's view, *we* are not called to imitate God at all or at least cannot be so called. If someone other than Moses imitates God as Moses did, then that person would, willy nilly, be founding a new ideal society, one which must in some way —if only in terms of the language in which it is conveyed and the historical events it recounts— be different from that of Moses. In other words, Berman's form of the imitation of God involves the creation of a new religion. We have two options here. We can either admit that this is the case or claim that Maimonides' statements about imitation of God in III 54 are directed only at Moses and at no one else at all. Neither option is acceptable. The first reads

Maimonides as if he were out to deny all his claims about the uniqueness of Mosaic prophecy and the immutability of the Torah.[22] It further gives a mile-wide opening to those who want to legitimate Jesus or Muhammad as prophets. One need hardly argue the point that this is not Maimonides' position! But one of the consequences of Berman's position is that he must in fact leave open this very possibility:

> Maimonides intimates that were Moses to come in his time, he would not need to lay down the sacrificial cult since the multitude in the time of Maimonides did not seem to be in need of this additional burden. This accords perfectly with the Alfarabian notion that were a philosopher-statesman of the same rank to come after the first founder of the religion, he would have the right to change the prescriptions of the first founder in accordance with the different circumstances current in his day. Here one receives an idea of religion which is flexible and seemingly malleable and responsive to the needs of the time.[23]

The second option —that III 54 is directed only at Moses— not only goes against the clearly expressed language and intent of the chapter but also involves us in the absurdity of maintaining that to the extent that Jews are called upon to imitate anybody, it is Moses, not God.

None of this, it should be noted, would be objectionable to Al-Farabi either because, as Rahman maintains, he had the image of Muhammad before him when he formulated his ideas concerning *imitatio Dei* or because, as Berman maintains, he adopted a view of religion characterized by flexibility and malleability. Neither option, however, is applicable to Maimonides: Muhammad's role in Islam is not isomorphic to that of Moses in Judaism and, Berman to the contrary, there is no evidence that Maimonides did not take with utter seriousness his claims concerning the unique character of Mosaic revelation. In short, to read Maimonides as Berman wants us to, we must transpose him from a Jewish into a Muslim context —and that seems a rather high price to pay, especially when the option of reading Maimonides as a Jew remains open to us— and interpret him as ultimately denying the unique character of Mosaic revelation.[24]

It will be useful, I think, to summarize very briefly the discussion to this point. I have shown that we are presented with two choices concerning the proper interpretation of Maimonides' views on the ultimate nature of human perfection: intellectual and practical. I have begun (and will continue below) to show that the second interpretation is superior to the first, with the proviso that proper practical perfection depends upon antecedent intellectual perfection.   But what sort of practical perfection? All agree that practical perfection involves the imitation of God. But how do we imitate God after having achieved intellectual perfection? Three separate views have been proposed. One view overemphasizes the political aspect of Maimonides' interpretation of the Torah and connects that view with a radically naturalistic reading of Maimonides. In this view, man's practical perfection rests in the creation of an ideal society and, unless we are willing to read Maimonides as a religious pluralist, we must say that only one human being has achieved the sort of perfection described in III 54: Moses. A second interpretation sees the imitation of God according to Maimonides as residing in moral behavior resting on the rational understanding that only thus are human beings truly human. The third approach, defended here, maintains that for Maimonides one most truly imitates God by fulfilling the commandments of the Torah out of love for God after achieving intellectual perfection.

By way of supporting this interpretation, I have presented a new interpretation of the parable of the palace, in which I show that in the parable Maimonides discusses human perfection *only* among Jews. This is not to say that for Maimonides gentiles cannot achieve human perfection; it is to say that in the present context the questions of to what extent and how gentiles achieve human perfection did not concern him. This interpretation leads us to see that the most perfected individuals (among Jews, at least, the objects of Maimonides' interest in the *Guide*) are experts in halakhah who have gone beyond halakhic competence to achieve perfection in physics and metaphysics and more. This position was further supported both by an analysis of Maimonides' comments on *imitatio Dei* in the *Guide* showing that in Maimonides' view one imitates God most truly by obeying the commandments and by a critique of the views of those who interpret Maimonides' practical perfection in moral or political terms.

Chapter Six

Imitatio Dei and Intellectual Perfection

Our discussion has brought us to the point where we can now raise two important and interrelated issues. What is the connection between the first chapters of the *Guide* and its last chapters, and what is the connection between intellectual perfection and imitation of God?

The first chapter of the *Guide* is devoted to an explication of the terms *zelem* and *demut* ("image" and "likeness"). It is in that context that Maimonides says (p. 23):

> Now man possesses as his proprium something in him that is very strange as it is not found in anything else that exists under the sphere of the moon, namely, intellectual apprehension. In the exercise of this, no sense, no part of the body, none of the extremities are used; and therefore this apprehension was likened unto the apprehension of the deity, which does not require an instrument, although in reality it is not like the latter apprehension, but only appears so to the first stirrings of opinion. It was because of this something, I mean because of the divine intellect conjoined with man, that it is said of the latter that he is *in the image of God and in His likeness*, not that God, may He be exalted, is a body and possesses a shape.

Maimonides tells us here that man's perfection *qua* man is something unique to him in the sublunar world. This perfection is intellectual apprehension. This apprehension, since it relies on no physical tools, has been mistakenly likened to God's apprehension. That, however, is incorrect, and "only appears so to the first stirrings of opinion." This apprehension, however, is still called "divine intellect" and is the reason that man is said to have been created in the image of God. But how can we be said to have been created in the image of God if that by virtue of which the Godlikeness in us exists is not really Godlike? Maimonides' claim seems to be that our Godlikeness consists of our intellectual apprehensions, which makes us like the supra-lunar Separate Intellects. That is the highest perfection to which we can aspire. We cannot become like God; we can, however, to some degree become like the Separate Intellects. It is in this sense, it appears, that we must read statements such as the following (I 2, p. 24):

For the intellect that God caused to emanate to man and that is man's ultimate perfection, was that which Adam was provided with before his disobedience. It was because of this that it was said of him that he was created *in the image of God and in His likeness.*

It is easy to misunderstand Maimonides' position here and read him as if he were maintaining that, since man is created in God's image and since that in man which makes this so is his intellect, God must have an intellect in some sense similar to that of man. The imitation of God, therefore, must involve the perfection of our intellect to the greatest extent possible, and nothing else.

As we have just seen, however, this is not what Maimonides actually says. Mankind's highest perfection is, indeed, intellectual. By perfecting our intellects we do indeed make ourselves fully human. But that is not the imitation of God, nor can it be. The imitation of God should not make us fully human, it should make us something more than fully human, it should make us in some sense Godlike. To say anything else is to drag God down to human level, not elevate humanity to something divine.

By perfecting our intellects, that is, by perfecting ourselves as human beings, we also earn (or, perhaps, create) our own immortality. The imitation of God, however, is something done purely out of love, not for any reward.[1] The very fact that Maimonides repeatedly links intellectual perfection to immortality should alert us to the fact that such perfection cannot be the highest state available to human beings, since the fact that an extrinsic reward is earned thereby (even if it is not strictly speaking a *reward* but a *consequence* of the activity) would seem to taint the purity of the love by which such states should be achieved.[2]

Now the *Guide* is meant to be exactly that: a guide. That being so, one should expect that the end of the book should reflect a reality different from that expressed at its beginning. Were this not so, the book would have to be considered a failure, since it would not in fact *guide* its readers from one state to another. The beginning of the book, therefore, should reflect a lower or less sophisticated vision of what people should strive for than the end of the book. That is exactly what we find: intellectual perfection is set up as the goal of humanity at the beginning of the book, while the book ends with the stirring call to imitate God through loving-kindness, righteousness, and judgment after intellectual perfection has been achieved.

In brief, intellectual perfection is indeed our highest perfection. But it is not, for all that, the imitation of God. That is an activity which we can aspire to perform in its fullest sense only after intellectual perfection has been achieved. *Imitatio Dei* in this fashion expresses love of God. This love is much more than intellectual perfection alone, since it finds its expression in action.

This is perhaps the best place to note the following important facts. The exposition of Maimonides offered here, even though it emphasizes Maimonides' view of the *mizvot* as the proper way for the intellectually perfected Jew to imitate God, would not be acceptable to rabbinic Judaism as it is ordinarily understood, since it affirms the superiority of intellectual perfection over simple obedience to the commandments, since it makes immortality conditional upon intellectual perfection, and since it denies that obedience to the commandments (whether by the vulgar without intellectual perfection or by the intellectually perfected) carries with it any reward over and above the carrying out of the *mizvot* themselves.[3] Second, it may very well be that Maimonides viewed intellectual perfection as the highest form of perfection open to gentiles (who know not the Torah), as opposed to the higher (if not more greatly rewarded) practical perfection open to Jews who know the Torah and who can therefore, imitate God properly.

Chapter Seven

Imitatio Dei and the Nature of God

It would seem that if man is to imitate God, then something of God's nature or activity must be known; otherwise, how can He be imitated? What, then, does Maimonides' doctrine of the imitation of God as presented here tell us about his doctrine of God?

Shlomo Pines has argued in a number of studies that Maimonides makes inconsistent statements about the nature of God in the *Guide*.[1] On the one hand, Maimonides teaches, or seems to teach, that God "is the intellect, as well as the intellectually cognizing subject and the intellectually cognized object, and that these three notions form in Him, may He be exalted, one single notion in which there is no multiplicity" (I 68, p. 163). Maimonides goes on here to point out that he had cited this fact about God in the *Mishneh Torah* and goes so far as to call it "one of the foundations of the Law." Pines argues that Maimonides' position here is tantamount to the claim that God is identical with the system of the sciences in the cosmos.[2] This carries with it the attendant consequence that God is in no sense to be construed as the personal Creator-God of Biblical religion. Whether or not Pines is right in this interpretation, it is indeed the case that if Maimonides can assert that God is Knowing, Knower, and Known, then he is affirming something positive about God. That something which he affirms positively of God (intellect) is something which we may be thought to have in common with God.[3]

This description of God has clear Aristotelian roots.[4] It also contradicts the view of God, derived from Neoplatonic sources,[5] that Maimonides teaches at such length and in such detail (I 51-60), that God, in and of Himself, is totally unknowable and that all we can actually know of Him are His actions. It is in this second view, and in this second view alone, that God an be said to create the world and govern it. In the first view, God must be accused of what Philo called "a vast inactivity."[6]

Now it happens that these two views of God correspond to the two sorts of human perfection and the two sorts of *imitatio Dei* which we have discussed in this study. If God is Knowing, Knower, and Known, that is, an intellect, then our imitation of God must be purely intellectual, and we can achieve the sort of imitation of God which I identified above as typical of the philosophical tradition: through the knowledge of philosophic truths we actually make ourselves *like* God.

On the other hand, if God in and of Himself is unknowable, then we can never make ourselves like God and the only way we can imitate Him is by "walking in His ways," that is, by performing certain actions. These actions, I have tried to show above, are not the dictates of morality as such nor are they the actions of a statesman founding a virtuous city; they are, rather, the actions which God prescribed in His Torah.

One can, however, reject my interpretation of the specific nature of the actions which must be undertaken in order to imitate God and still agree that if we take III 54 and not I 1 as determining Maimonides' final position, then we must imitate God through His actional attributes (however they are perceived). If we take this to be the final teaching of the *Guide* (perhaps the fact that it is literally the *final* teaching of the *Guide* indicates that it is indeed the final teaching of the work), then we are led to claim that in the end Maimonides adopts the Neoplatonic view of the hidden God, known only by His actions, and rejects the Aristotelian view of God as intellect. In this interpretation, Maimonides' God is most certainly not to be identified with the system of the sciences.

How are we to understand this? Are the two different views of God which appear to be expressed in the *Guide* a contradiction which Maimonides failed to resolve? Was he torn between two views of God, one which appealed to his intellect and the other to his religious sense? Are we perhaps witness here to a development in Maimonides' views? None of these proposed solutions is attractive, because they all accuse Maimonides of a sloppiness of thought and expression which is rare and perhaps altogether absent from his writings.

All this, I think, meshes well with what I said above about the *Guide of the Perplexed* actually being a guide of the perplexed. We may indeed be witnesses here to a kind of development, not in Maimonides' thought, but, rather, a hoped-for development in the reader of the *Guide*, whereby Maimonides tries to wean those capable of being weaned from a hackneyed philosophical position (God = Intellect) and lead them to a more sophisticated religio-philosophical position (God as object of worship and model for imitation insofar as humans can imitate Him).

Chapter Eight

Summary and Conclusions

I have attempted to present a reading of Maimonides' comments on the nature of human perfection which shows that the highest perfection available to Jews is the imitation of God through the observance of the commandments of the Torah. To the extent that I have succeeded in showing the reasonableness of this interpretation of Maimonides, I have also shown the reasonableness of interpreting Maimonides as a Jew who accepted as true the claim that God revealed the Torah to the Jewish people through Moses at Sinai and who therefore saw the observance of the commandments of the Torah as something of ultimate importance. To the extent that I have shown that this interpretation of Maimonides is convincing, I have weakened an alternative interpretation which sees Maimonides as adopting positions which he knows to be at variance with what the Torah truly teaches. This latter position insists that Maimonides denies the personal creator-God of biblical religion in favor of the philosophical-God of Aristotelian philosophy. I have noted also, and it is important to re-emphasize, that even in my interpretation, Maimonides' position is not acceptable to almost all adherents of rabbinic Judaism as it is ordinarily understood. I have not, that is to say, been attempting to read Maimonides as a standard bearer for Jewish "orthodoxy," either as it was received in his day or as it developed after him. Last, I do not delude myself that I have *proved* anything. We have before us a man and a text. I have done my best to read that text in the light of what we know about the man. That is a difficult job even with texts the meaning of which is as transparent as can be. It is much, much more difficult with a text purposefully written so as to obscure the author's intentions.[1]

I should like now to summarize the main points of my exposition. In the first chapter, I adduced texts from a variety of Maimonides' works which indicate that for human beings "ultimate perfection is to become rational in actu." Man's *summum bonum*, that is, is intellectual perfection. In most of these texts, Maimonides also maintains that intellectual perfection is the only route to immortality.

In Chapter II, I introduced the well-known text from the end of the *Guide of the Perplexed* (III 54), in which Maimonides maintains that the most perfect individuals apprehend God to the greatest extent possible to

61

them. Having achieved this level of apprehension, they then realize that they ought to seek to emulate God's loving-kindness, righteousness, and judgment. How does one emulate God in this fashion? We find three main approaches discussed in the literature on Maimonides: one imitates God after intellectual perfection, it is maintained, either by acting morally, by founding just states, or by obeying His commandments.

Chapter III is given over to an exposition of *Guide* III 51-54. In this exposition, I try to show that intellectual perfection is not the highest state open to human beings. This highest state consists of practical action of a certain kind in the world after one has achieved intellectual perfection. It is through this practice that one imitates God to the extent that God can be imitated by human beings. I further attempt to show that the kind of practical action which Maimonides envisioned here is observance of God's commands as found in the Torah.

One of the more important elements of this exposition is, to the best of my knowledge, a new interpretation of Maimonides' parable of the palace (III 51). In this interpretation, the parable deals with the levels of perfection open to Jews, not to human beings in general. I suggest that the various levels of perfection described in the parable--simple obedience to the commandments of the Torah, competence in halakhah, knowledge of the principles of religion and of physics, expertise in metaphysics, prophecy, and Mosaic prophecy--depends each upon its predecessor and refers to a smaller group of people: each class, that is, is a subset of the class before it, maintains the perfection of that class, and adds to it its own particular perfection. This being so, if the parable starts with Jews, it must end with Jews. If it starts with Jews committed to halakhic obedience, it ends with Jews so committed. The intellectualism valued by the parable of the palace, therefore, is an intellectualism built upon a firm foundation of halakhah. One would expect to find some expression of this footing, suitably revalued, in the life of the perfected.

In my exposition of the rest of the chapters of this concluding section of the *Guide*, I attempt to show that for Maimonides the highest level of contemplation should be joined with a kind of social activity, namely, the "bringing into being of a religious community that would know and worship God." This end, even though it clearly has a political aspect, is best realized through the imitation of God through obedience to His commandments.

Our reading of the last four chapters of the *Guide* leads to two conclusions: (a) intellectual perfection alone is not the "be-all-and-end-all" of human life; and (b) *after* achieving intellectual perfection, Jews ought to imitate God through the fulfillment of the commandments of the Torah.

This being the case, the question boils down to how we imitate God, the subject of Chapter IV. I suggest that Maimonides sees *imitatio Dei*, not in terms of our actually becoming like God, but in terms of our patterning our actions after God's actions. Here, one's understanding of Maimonides' view of God is crucial. Imitation of a purely intellectual God is vastly different from the imitation of a creator-God who knows His creatures and provides for them. I attempt to show textually that Maimonides consistently explains *imitatio Dei* in terms of obedience to the commandments. Halakhah, that is to say, is the way in which God has commanded the Jews to imitate Him.

In Chapter V, I turn to a criticism of the moral and political interpretations of practical perfection. I suggest that Maimonides' deprecation of morality *vis-á-vis* intellectual perfection makes it unlikely that he would see in morality as such the highest practical perfection of the Jew. I further suggest that if, by "morality", some of Maimonides' interpreters mean "obedience to God's commands" then they ought to say that and not confuse the issue by adopting terminology which Maimonides explicitly rejects. With respect to the political interpretation, I show that its adherents connect it with a radically naturalistic (in our terms, secularist) reading of Maimonides, a reading which appears to me to be inconsistent with the facts of Maimonides' life as we know them. The credibility of that reading is, moreover, seriously weakened to the extent that my exposition of III 51-54 is convincing. I further indicate that the political interpretation of human perfection as it has been presented reads Maimonides in much too Muslim a light and either restricts practical perfection to Moses (and this is at variance with the straightforward sense of Maimonides' statements) or opens the possibility that others might emulate God by establishing just societies as did Moses (and who is to say that their names might not be Jesus or Muhammad?).

In the following Chapter (VI), I take up the question, What is the connection between intellectual perfection and the imitation of God? I suggest that the highest perfection which human beings *qua* human beings can aspire to is intellectual perfection. But that is not the final obligation to which humans are subject, since perfecting our intellects is not the imitation of God. But we cannot imitate God in and of Himself, nor can we actually imitate His actions (how many of us create worlds and provide for their inhabitants?). What we can do is imitate God as we are instructed to by the Torah. This imitation, done with no thought of reward, is the truest expression of the pure love of God available to us.

In Chapter VII, I suggest that from what we have learned here about the imitation of God, we can infer something about Maimonides' view of the nature of God. The *Guide*, I suggest, is exactly that, *a guide* leading us from the view of God as intellect, whom we emulate by contemplation, to the view of God as active in the world, whom we emulate through performance of His commandments. Maimonides' book is transformative and not simply expository, subsuming throughout a practical aim.

Notes

Chapter One

[1]Berakhot 17a.

[2] In the sequel Maimonides explains that God is the object of cognition which grants immortality. Given the limitations Maimonides places on the possibility of our cognizing God (see Shlomo Pines, "The Limitations of Human Knowledge According to Al-Farabi, ibn Bajja, and Maimonides," I. Twersky [ed.], *Studies in Medieval Jewish History and Literature* [Cambridge: Harvard University Press, 1979]: 82-109 —henceforth, "Limitations"), it is not easy to understand what he means by this. But even if intellectual perfection cannot be achieved through positive knowledge of God, that does not mean that we do not perfect ourselves by learning more and more of what God is not. Intellectual perfection in the sense of acquiring true positive knowledge of God may not be available to us; that does not mean that no intellectual perfection is available to us. See Warren Zev Harvey, *"Bein Philosophiah Medinit li-Halakhah bi-Mishnat ha-Rambam,"* *Iyyun* 29 (1980): 198-212, appendix.

[3] Lit.: "it and it are the same thing." Maimonides is referring to the identity of the knower and the object known. See Aristotle, *Metaphysics* XII 9; *Guide of the Perplexed,* translated by Shlomo Pines (Chicago: University of Chicago Press, 1963), I 68 (pp. 163-4; henceforth all citations to the *Guide* will be to this edition; I have introduced emendations into Pines' translation, following suggestions made to me in this matter by Lenn Evan Goodman, for whose assistance I am most grateful); and Pines, "Limitations," pp. 91 and 93.

[4] *Mishnah im Perush Rabbenu Mosheh ben Maimon,* ed. and trans. by J. Kafih (Jerusalem: Mossad ha-Rav Kook, 1963), Vol. IV (Nezikin): 205 (the text appears in Maimonides' "Introduction to *Helek*"); in the same edition, see also Vol. I, p. 44, where the intellect is called "man's divine faculty." See also the beginning of the fifth of Maimonides' "Eight Chapters": "Man needs to subordinate all his soul's powers to thought. . . .and to set his sight on a single goal: the perception of God. . . .I mean, knowledge of Him, in so far as that lies within man's power." I quote from the translation in Weiss and Butterworth (eds.), *Ethical Writings of Maimonides* (New York: Dover, 1983): 75.

[5]I.e., the intellect.

[6]I quote from the translation of Moses Hyamson, Maimonides, *The Book of Knowledge* (New York: Feldheim, 1974): 39a. See also Harry Austryn Wolfson, *The Philosophy of Spinoza* (Cambridge: Harvard University Press, 1934), II: 290-291.

[7]As with so many other issues, Maimondes' actual position on the acquired intellect is not entirely clear. See Warren Zev Harvey, "Hasdai Crescas' Critique of the Theory of the Acquired Intellect," Ph.D. Diss. (Columbia University, 1973; Xerox University Microfilms order no. 74-1488): 28-29 and 40-44; and Harvey, "*R. Hasdai Crescas u-Vikorto al ha-Osher ha-Philosophi*," *Proceedings of the Sixth World Congress of Jewish Studies* (Jerusalem: World Congress of Jewish Studies, 1977), III: 143-9. On the Separate Intellects in Maimonides, see *Guide* II 2-12; Zvi (Harry) Blumberg, "*Ha-Sekhalim ha-Nivdalim bi-Mishnato shel ha-Rambam*," *Tarbiz* 40 (1971): 216-225; and Joseph Heller, "*Mahuto vi-Tafkido shel ha-Sekhel ha-Poel lifi Torat ha-Rambam*," in S. Bernstein and G. Churgin (eds.), *S. K. Mirsky Jubilee Volume* (New York, 1958): 26-42.

[8]"Laws of Repentance," VIII 3; Hyamson, pp. 90a-b.

[9]"Laws of Tefilin, Mezuzah and Sefer Torah," VI 13.

[10]Avot I 17. Compare Avot III 12 and 22 and IV 6, Berakhot 17a and Ketubot 77a. See E. E. Urbach, *The Sages: Their Concepts and Beliefs* (Jerusalem: Magnes Press, 1975), chapter 16, section 7. For an interesting sidelight, see Harry Austryn Wolfson, *The Philosophy of the Church Fathers*, 3rd ed. rev. (Cambridge: Harvard University Press, 1970): 100.

[11]Shlomo Pines, "Translator's Introduction: The Philosophic Sources of *The Guide of the Perplexed*" in his translation of the *Guide* (Chicago: University of Chicago Press, 1963): cxix (henceforth, "Introduction").

[12]P. 63.

[13]Lit., "conception."

[14]Here and throughout, this might be better rendered as "entelechy."

[15]Here we see that Maimonides denies that we will have new cognitions after death. It is in light of this passage, I think, that we ought to read the following passage from "Laws of Repentance," VIII 3: "And what is the meaning of the sages' statement, 'they enjoy the radiance of the Shechinah'? It means that the righteous attain a knowledge and realization of the truth concerning God to which they had not attained while they were in the murky and lowly body."

[16]Pp. 627-8. For a study of Maimonides' statements on the love of God, see Georges Vajda, *L'amour de Dieu dans la theologie juive du moyen age* (Paris: Vrin, 1957): 118-40. On death by a kiss see Moshe Idel, *The Mystical Experience in Abraham Abulafia* (Albany: SUNY Press, 1988): 180-84.

[17]Proverbs 5:17.

[18]P. 635. Further support for this approach to Maimonides may be found in the emphasis he places on the importance and value of solitude. See, for example, II 36 (p. 372): and III 51 (p. 621). See also below, chapter three, note 62.

[19]Further in this vein, see Maimonides' comment in his "Letter on Resurrection," in Y. Kafih (ed.): *Iggerot ha-Rambam* (Jerusalem: Mossad ha-Rav Kook, 1972): 73, on the importance of the knowledge of God. See further Maimonides' letter to R. Hasdai ha-Levi in *Kovez Teshuvot ha-Rambam vi-Iggerotav* (Leipzig, 1859 [reprinted in Jerusalem, 1967]): Vol. II 23d-24a: "As for what you ask about the gentile nations, you must know that God asks for the heart [a reference to Sanhedrin 106b], and things go according to the heart's intention. Therefore, the sages of truth, our rabbis, may they rest in peace, said: 'the righteous of the gentile nations of the world have a share in the world to come' —*if they have attained that which it is proper to attain of the knowledge of the Creator, blessed be He* and have improved their souls with virtuous qualities [*middot ha-tovot*]. There is no doubt that everyone who has improved his soul with the propriety of the virtues and with the propriety of wisdom in the faith in the Creator, blessed be He, is certainly among the children of the world to come. . . ." I quote the text with minor changes and with emphasis added from Steven Schwarzschild, "Do Noachites Have to Believe in Revelation?" *JQR* 52 (1962): 297-398, and 53 (1962): 30-65. The passage in question appears on p. 39.

[20]See, for example, Isaac Husik, *A History of Medieval Jewish Philosophy* (New York: MacMillan, 1930): 299-300; Pines, "Introduction," p. cxxi; and Alexander Altmann, "Maimonides' 'Four Perfections'," *Israel Oriental Studies* 2 (1972): 15-24, reprinted with additions in Altmann, *Essays in Jewish Intellectual History* (Hanover, N.H.: University Press of New England, 1981): 65-76. See also Harry (Zvi): Blumberg, "The Problem of Immortality in Avicenna, Maimonides and St. Thomas Aquinas," *Harry Austryn Wolfson Jubilee Volume* (Jerusalem: American Academy for Jewish Research, 1965): 165-85 (reprinted in Jacob I. Dienstag [ed.], *Studies in Maimonides and St. Thomas Aquinas* [New York: Ktav Publishing House, 1975]: 29-49.) Further on Maimonides' intellectualist stance, see Haim (Howard) Kreisel, "*Zaddik vi-Ra Lo ba-Philosophiah ha-Yehudit bimei ha-Benayim*," *Da'at* 19 (1987): 17-29, note 28. For an interpretation of Maimonides' intellectualism in mystical

terms, see David R. Blumenthal, "Maimonides' Intellectualist Mysticism and the Superiority of the Prophecy of Moses," *Studies in Medieval Culture* 10 (1978): 51-67. It should be noted that whether or not Blumenthal is correct in seeing Maimonides' intellectualism in mystical terms has no bearing on the position defended in this study. For a medieval Jewish view of human perfection in strictly intellectualist terms by a faithful student of Maimonides, see Raphael Jospe's study of Shem Tov ibn Falaquera, "Rejecting Moral Virtue as the Ultimate Human End," in William Brinner and Stephen Ricks (eds.): *Studies in Islamic and Jewish Traditions* (Denver: University of Denver, 1986): 185-204. Samuel ibn Tibbon was also strict in seeing human perfection in intellectual terms and even criticized Maimonides for appearing to abandon this position at the end of the *Guide*. See Aviezer Ravitzky, "Samuel ibn Tibbon and the Esoteric Character of the *Guide of the Perplexed*," *AJSReview* 6 (1981): 87-123, esp. p. 122.

Chapter Two

[1]Leo Strauss may be credited with having raised the issue of Maimonides' esotericism in modern scholarship. See "The Literary Character of the *Guide of the Perplexed*," in S. W. Baron (ed.), *Essays on Maimonides* (New York: Columbia University Press, 1941): 37-91 (reprinted in Strauss, *Persecution and the Art of Writing* [Glencoe, Illinois: Free Press, 1976]: 3-94); "How to Begin to Study the *Guide of the Perplexed*," in Pines' translation of the *Guide*, pp. xi-lvi. His earlier studies on the subject are encapsulated in the recently translated *Philosophy and Law* (Philadelphia: Jewish Publication Society, 1987). Strauss' influence on Pines is evident in his "Translator's Introduction" and in the "Excursus" (pp. 195-8) to his "Abul-Barakat's Poetics and Metaphysics," *Scripta Hiersolymitana* 6 (Jerusalem, 1960): 120-98. Further on this issue, see: Joseph Buijs, "The Philosophical Character of Maimonides' *Guide*—A Critique of Strauss' Interpretation," *Judaism* 27 (1978): 448-57; David Hartman, *Maimonides: Torah and Philosophic Quest* (Philadelphia: Jewish Publication Society, 1976), "Introduction"; Warren Zev Harvey, "The Return of Maimonideanism," *Journal of Jewish Social Studies* 42 (1980): 249-68; Arthur Hyman, "Interpreting Maimonides," *Gesher* 5 (1976): 46-59; Oliver Leaman, "Does the Interpretation of Islamic Philosophy Rest on a Mistake?" *International Journal of Middle East Studies* 12

(1980): 525-38. This article was reprinted as the last chapter of Leaman's *Introduction to Medieval Islamic Philosophy* (Cambridge: Cambridge University Press, 1985) and was subjected to a scathing critique by Charles Butterworth in "On Scholarship and Scholarly Conventions," *Journal of the American Oriental Society* 106 (1986): 725-32; Aryeh Leo Motzkin, "On the Interpretation of Maimonides," *International Journal of Philosophy* 2 (1978): 39-46; see also the article by Aviezer Ravitzky cited in chapter 1, note 20, and his recent *"Sitrei Torato shel 'Moreh ha-Nevukhim': ha-Parshanut bi-Dorotav u-vi-Doroteinu,"* *Jerusalem Studies in Jewish Thought* 5 (1987): 23-69. Not strictly relevant to his reading of Maimonides, but interesting for the light it throws on Strauss himself, is the essay by S. B. Drury, "The Esoteric Philosophy of Leo Strauss," *Political Theory* 13 (1985): 315-37. For a recent critique of Strauss' reading of Maimonides, see Marvin Fox, "A New View of Maimonides' Method of Contradictions," in Moshe Hallamish (ed.), *Bar Ilan: Annual of Bar Ilan University — Studies in Judaica and the Humanities* 22-23 (Moshe Schwarcz Memorial Volume) (Ramat Gan: Bar Ilan University Press, 1987): 19-43. Further on Strauss' reading of Maimonides, see Charles M. Raffel, "Providence as Consequent Upon the Intellect: Maimonides' Theory of Providence," *AJSReview* 12 (1987): 25-71, esp. p. 28.

[2]See Abraham Melamed's exhaustive survey, *"Al Yithalel — Perushim Philosophi'im li-Yirmiyahu 9: 22-23 ba-Mahshavah ha-Yehudit bi-Yimei ha-Benayim vi-ha-Renaissance,"* *Jerusalem Studies in Jewish Thought* 4 (1985): 31-82.

[3]See Hermann Cohen, *"Ofyah shel Torat Ha-Middot li-ha-Rambam,"* in Cohen's *Iyyunim bi-Yahadut u-vi-Ba'ayot ha-Dor* (Jerusalem: Mossad Bialik, 1978): 17-59 (a Hebrew translation of Cohen's "Charakteristik der Ethik Maimunis," from W. Bacher, *et al.* [eds.], *Moses ben Maimon* [Leipzig, 1908], I, 63-134); Julius Guttmann, *Philosophies of Judaism* (New York: Schocken Books, 1973): 200-3; Guttmann, "Introduction and Commentary", *The Guide of the Perplexed: An Abridged Edition*, translated by Chaim Rabin (London: East and West Library, 1947): 34, 225; and Steven Schwarzschild, "Moral Radicalism and 'Middlingness' in the Ethics of Maimonides," *Studies in Medieval Culture* 11 (1977): 65-94. For variants of this position, see Zvi Diesendruck, "Die Teleologie bei Maimonides," *HUCA* 5 (1928): 415-535, and *"Ha-Takhlit vi-ha-Toarim bi-Torat ha-Rambam,"* *Tarbiz* 1 (1930): 106-36, and 2 (1931): 27-73 (reprinted in *Likkutei Tarbiz 5: Mikra'ah bi-Heker ha-Rambam* [Jerusalem: Magnes Press, 1985]: 187-264); and Daniel H. Frank, "The End of the Guide: Maimonides on the Best Life for Man," *Judaism* 34 (1985): 485-95.

[4]See the studies by Strauss, cited above in note 1, and the following studies by Lawrence V. Berman: *"Ibn Bajja vi-ha-Rambam,"* Ph.D. Diss.

(Hebrew University, 1959), chapter 1; "Maimonides, the Disciple of Alfarabi," *Israel Oriental Studies* 4 (1974): 154-78; "The Political Interpretation of the Maxim: The Purpose of Philosophy is the Imitation of God," *Studia Islamica* 15 (1961): 53-61; "Maimonides on the Fall of Man," *AJSReview* 5 (1980): 1-15; and "Maimonides on Political Leadership," in Daniel J. Elazar (ed.), *Kinship and Consent* (Ramat Gan: Turtledove Publishing, 1981): 113-25.

[5]See above, note 3.

[6]J. Guttmann, *Philosophies of Judaism* (see above, note 3):   200. Guttmann, it is true, faults Cohen for, in effect, presenting Maimonides as a proto-Kantian (pp. 404-6), but that does not stop him from following Cohen's neo-Kantian reading of Maimonides' account of the place of ethics in human perfection.

[7]See Schwarzschild's essay, cited above in note 3.

[8]See above, notes 1 and 4.

[9]Pines, "Limitations," p. 100. See also Pines' latest statement on the subject, "The Philosophical Purport of Maimonides' Halachic Works and the Purport of *The Guide of the Perplexed*," in S. Pines and Y. Yovel (eds.), *Maimonides and Philosophy* (Dordrecht: Martinus Nijhoff, 1986): 1-14. Alexander Altmann presents a different reading of Maimonides in his posthumous "Maimonides on the Intellect and the Scope of Metaphysics," in his *Von der mittelalterlichen zur modernen Aufklaerung* (Tuebingen: JCB Mohr, 1986): 60-129.

[10]Isadore Twersky, *Introduction to the Code of Maimonides* (New Haven: Yale University Press, 1980), p. 511. See also Twersky, "Some Non-Halakic Aspects of the Mishneh Torah," in Alexander Altmann (ed.), *Jewish Medieval and Renaissance Studies* (Cambridge: Harvard University Press, 1967): 161-82; reprinted in Twersky's *Studies in Jewish Law and Philosophy* (New York: Ktav, 1982): 52-75.

[11]David Hartman (above, this chapter, note 1), p. 26. For a further and very clear expression of the position under discussion here, see also Shalom Rosenberg, "Ethics," in Arthur A. Cohen and Paul Mendes-Flohr (eds.), *Contemporary Jewish Religious Thought* (New York: Scribners, 1987): 195-202. In connection with Maimonides at the end of III 54, Rosenberg writes, "The imitation of God, the walking in his ways, is thus the highest norm determining the Jew's actions. More precisely it is a meta-ethical principle from which religious statutes or *halakhot* —literally, ways of walking— are derived. Here *the way* is emphasized. In another sense the imitation of God is seen not as a commandment, but as a goal and a promise. A resemblance to God is promised as a state to be attained

in the End of Days and as the goal of personal salvation" (p. 201). There
is, of course, no conflict between the two interpretations of Maimonides
offered here by Rosenberg.

Chapter Three

[1]For a recent and most valuable study of Maimonides on "ta'amei
ha-mizvot" (reasons for the commandments), see Josef Stern, "The Idea
of a Hoq in Maimonides' Explanation of the Law," in S. Pines and Y.
Yovel (eds.), Maimonides and Philosophy (Dordrecht: Martinus Nijhoff,
1986): 92-130. In addition to the sources cited by Stern, see also Hannah
Kasher, "Maimonides' Philosophical Division of the Laws," HUCA 56
(1985): 1-7 (Hebrew section).

[2] See, for example, Isaac Abravanel's discussion in Haslat Abravanel...
published at the end of many editions of the Guide; Shem Tov's comment
at the end of his commentary to III 51; Leo Strauss' introduction to Pines'
translation of the Guide, p. xiii, and his "Maimonides' Statement on
Political Science," PAAJR 22 (1953): 115-30 (p. 126); Lawrence V.
Berman, "The Structure of Maimonides' Guide of the Perplexed,"
Proceedings of the Sixth World Congress of Jewish Studies, III (Jerusalem:
World Union of Jewish Studies, 1977) 12; and Menachem Marc Kellner,
"Maimonides' 'Thirteen Principles' and the Structure of the Guide for the
Perplexed," Journal of the History of Philosophy 20 (1982): 76-84. This
position is also held by Vajda (see above, chapter one, note 16), p. 133.

[3]On p. 620, Maimonides defines worship in terms equivalent to setting
thought "to work on God alone."

[4]In his Introduction, Maimonides defines the purpose of the Guide in the
following way: "The first purpose of this Treatise is to explain the
meanings of certain terms occurring in books of prophecy" (p. 5). "This
Treatise also has a second purpose: namely, the explanation of very
obscure parables occurring in the books of the prophets, but not explicitly
identified there as such" (p. 6). See also Guide II 2 (pp. 253-4) and Strauss
in his introduction to Pines' translation (above, chapter two, note 1), p.
xiv. On the link between III 51 and the preceding chapters, see Josef Stern
(above, note 1), p. 122f, who agrees with my contention that III 51 must

be read in the light of the immediately preceding section of the *Guide*, but, apparently disagrees with my claim that III 51-4 represents a distinct thematic unit (see this chapter, note 2).

[5]It is strange, then, that it is not the last chapter of the book. Compare Pines, "The Philosophic Purport. . ." (above, chapter two, note 9): 9.

[6]These being the three subjects which bring one to perfection. See the text cited above from III 8 (p. 437).

[7]While my attempts to avoid sexist usages reflect my own agenda and not that of Maimonides, it should still be noted that such usage can be justified in terms of Maimonides' own position on the possibility of women achieving intellectual perfection. Note his linkage of Miriam with Aaron and Moses in *Guide* III 51 (pp. 627-8) and his comments in "Laws of Repentance," X 1, on the possibility of educating women to worship God out of love and not just out of fear.

[8]Note that my interpretation here contradicts Maimonides' implied claim (p. 624) that his discussion of providence in III 51 was the result of a sudden inspiration which came to him while he was writing the chapter. Note also that I do not think that there is any contradiction between Maimonides' discussion of providence here and his discussion in III 17. There Maimonides discusses providence for "normal" people; here, providence for the "special worshipper." For other views, see Zvi Diesendruck, "Samuel and Moses ibn Tibbon on Maimondies' Theory of Providence," *HUCA* 11 (1936): 341-66, and Charles M. Raffel (above, chapter two, note 1).

[9]On p. 126 of his "Maimonides' Statement on Political Science" (this chapter, note 2), Leo Strauss maintains that Maimonides actually offers two different interpretations of the parable. I conflate the two, seeing the second as an amplification of the first. Strauss would have us believe that Maimonides offers two different interpretations of the parable in adjoining paragraphs. That is hard to swallow. See also below, note 26.

[10]I.e., physics.

[11]It interesting that Maimonides uses the singular here.

[12]This is the sort of text which warms the hearts of those who interpret Maimonides' views on perfection in political terms. God's governance of human beings, however, turns out to be expressed in terms of His loving-kindness, righteousness, and judgment, which are as much halakhic categories as they are political categories.

[13]Shem Tov ben Joseph ibn Shem Tov, *Commentary on the Guide of the Perplexed*, at III 51.

[14]Efodi is quoted by Shem Tov *ad loc*. I have not found the "introduction" Shem Tov refers to in any of the microfilmed mss. of Efodi's commentary on the *Guide* held by the Institute for Microfilmed Hebrew Manuscripts at the Jewish National and University Library in Jerusalem. For Falaquera, see his *Moreh ha-Moreh* (Pressburg, 1837 [reprinted in *Sheloshah Kadmonei Meforshei ha-Moreh*, Jerusalem, 1961]) 132.

[15]I refer, of course, to Strauss, Pines, and Berman. For a consistent and radically naturalistic reading of Maimonides, see Pines, "Translator's Introduction" and, phrased more cautiously, his article on Maimonides in the *Encyclopedia of Philosophy* (New York: MacMillan, 1967), V: 129-34. Lest I be accused of attacking a straw man, or of flogging a dead horse, or of other metaphorical atrocities, let it be noted that in his "Introduction," Pines, directly or indirectly, attributes the following views to Maimonides: that Moses may have been more of a philosopher than a prophet (p. lxxxviii); that there might be "no essential difference among monotheistic prophetic religions" (p. xc); that Maimonides did not believe in "freedom of man's will and action" as these terms are ordinarily understood (p. xcv); that God is nothing other than "the scientific system of the universe" and that as such may be equivalent to Spinoza's "attribute of thought" (p. xcviii; see also p. cxv); that there is no individual immortality (pp. cii-ciii) (on the implications of this denial, see Seymour Feldman's introduction to his translation of Levi ben Gerson, *Wars of the Lord* I [Philadelphia: Jewish Publication Society, 1984] 40): that God is the soul of the world (p. cxiv); that God is the first (and highest) of the separate intellects (pp. cxiv-cxv); that Maimonides' halakhic pursuits were nothing more than an "avocation" (!!!) (p. cxvii); that the prophets may not really have been philosophers after all (p. cxx); and that the claim that philosophic science flourished among the Jews of antiquity was a "convenient fiction" (p.cxxxiii) (consider the implications of this claim for Maimonides' assertions about the identity of *Ma'aseh Bereshit* with physics and of *Ma'aseh Merkavah* with metaphysics).

[16] See Deut. 20:16-18, Maimonides' "Laws of Kings and Their Wars," V 1 and 4, and *Guide* I 36 (p. 84) and I 54 (p. 127).

[17] See Deut. 13:13-18 and "Laws of Idolatry," IV.

[18] See Deut. 13:7-12 and "Laws of Idolatry," V 1-5.

[19] See the end of Maimonides' Thirteen Principles (see chapter 1, note 4), "Laws of Idolatry," X 1, "Laws of the Murderer," IV 10, and "Laws of Testimony," XI 10. Note should be taken of the fact that the obligation

to destroy *Amalek* (Deut. 25:17-19; *Book of Commandments*, positive commandment number 188; "Laws of Kings and Their Wars," I 1, V 5, and VI 4; and *Guide* III 41 [p. 566] and III 50 [p. 614-15]) does not fall under our purview here, since *Amalek* is to be destroyed for what it did, and not because of views adopted by the Amalekites.

[20]"Laws of Kings and Their Wars," V 4.

[21]"Laws of Kings and Their Wars," V 5: "So too, it is a positive command to destroy the memory of Amalek, as it is said, *Thou shalt blot out the remembrance of Amalek* (Deut. 25:19). It is a positive command always to bear in mind his evil deeds, the waylaying (he resorted to), so that we keep fresh the memory of the hatred manifested by him. . . ." (I cite, here and below, from the translation of A. M. Hershman, *The Book of Judges* [New Haven: Yale University Press, 1949], p. 217). There is no historicization here.

[22]But see *Book of Commandments*, positive commandment no. 187.

[23]The reference here is to the seven Noahide commandments, on which see David Novak, *The Image of the Non-Jew in Judaism* (New York: Mellen, 1983).

[24]Hershman, p. 230.

[25]"Laws of Kings," VIII 11 (Hershman, p. 230).

[26]For a reading of Maimonides' parable which supports the interpretation here presented —without by any means intending to do so!— see Pines, "Translator's Introduction," p. cxv f. Pines and I both understand Maimonides' second interpretation of the parable as coming to amplify the first, not replace it. See above, this chapter, note 9.

[27]Arabic: *Al-fuqaha*.

[28]I refer those who argue that Mosaic prophecy is not a form of prophecy to my *Dogma in Medieval Jewish Thought* (Oxford: Oxford University Press, 1986): 229 (henceforth, *Dogma*).

[29]The importance of order and symmetry to Maimonides is something assumed by nearly all of Maimonides' interpreters from Shem Tov and Abravanel (both of whom are concerned with investigating the architectonics of the *Guide*) to Leo Strauss. See, for example, his "Maimonides' Statement on Political Science" (this chapter, note 2): 125-6.

[30]See David R. Blumenthal, *The Commentary of R. Hoter ben Shelomoh to the Thirteen Principles of Maimonides* (Leiden: Brill, 1974): 52, note 2; and my *Dogma*: 17.

[31]In the edition of R. Kafih (see above, chapter one, note 4), pp. 205 and 210. See also my *Dogma*: 18.

[32]There is no evidence that Maimonides ever adopted such a position. On the sort of position I am *not* attributing to Maimonides here, see Ya'akov Katz, *Halakhah vi-Kabbalah* (Jerusalem: Magnes Press, 1974): 291-310.

[33]Thus, for example, "Laws of the Foundations *[yesodei]* of the Torah" comes at the beginning of the *Book of Knowledge*, a book which Maimonides characterizes as dealing with "the *ikkar* of religion" *(Mishneh Torah*, Introduction, at the end of the list of commandments and just before the table of contents).

[34]Maimonides uses the term "foundations of the Torah" *(qawa'id al shariah)* in the *Guide* for creation (I 71, p. 182; II 13, p. 282; II 23, p. 321; II 29, p. 346; III 50, p. 613), for the doctrine that God's knowledge of future contingent events does not destroy their contingent nature (III 17, p. 469; III 20, p. 482; III 32, p. 529), for the doctrine of the limits of the love and fear of God (III 24, p. 500), for the doctrine that prophets consider their prophecies to be true (III 24, pp. 500-1), and for what the Torah teaches concerning the existence of angels (II 2, p. 253; in support of this interpretation, see Rabbi Kafih's note there in his edition of the *Guide* [Jerusalem: Mossad ha-Rav Kook, 1972], p. 170). For other uses of the term "foundations" *(qawa'id)* ,see the Introduction (pp. 5 and 10), I 28 (p. 60), I 33 (p. 71), I 68 (p. 163), I 71 (pp. 177 and 179), II 24 (p. 323), II 25 (p. 328), II 39 (p. 379), III 17 (p. 471), III 18 (pp. 475 and 476), III 23 (p. 497), III 24 (p. 502), and III 45 (p. 576). The term "principles" *(usul)* appears at I 18 (p. 45), I 71 (pp. 176 and 181), II 2 (p. 254), II 24 (p. 326), II 33 (p. 364), and our own text, III 51 (p. 619).

[35]See S. Muntner (ed.), *Pirkei Mosheh* (Jerusalem: Mossad ha-Rav Kook, 1959): 381; and J. Kafih (ed.), *Iggerot ha-Rambam* (Jerusalem: Mossad ha-Rav Kook, 1972): 159.

[36]See Kafih (previous note): 148n and p. 159n.

[37]See L. V. Berman, "Structure," this chapter, note 2, p. 13n.

[38]The singularly Jewish character of the *Guide* is attested to by Maimonides' definition of its purpose (see this chapter, note 4), by its content, by the sources it cites, by the fact that it was written in Hebrew characters, and by the fact that Maimonides wanted to see it translated

into Hebrew. All this is independent of the question debated by Strauss (in his introduction to the Pines translation, p. xiv) and Buijs (see above, chapter two, note 1) concerning the philosophic character of the book. On the fact that the *Guide* was written in Hebrew characters, see p. 340 of Lawrence V. Berman, "Some Remarks on the Arabic Text of Maimonides' 'Treatise on the Art of Logic,'" *Journal of the American Oriental Society* 88 (1968): 340-2 and the sources cited there.

[39]See Twersky's "Some Non-Halakic Aspects. . . .": 106-18 (pp. 63-75 in the reprint) and his *Introduction to the Mishneh Torah*: 473-9 and 488-507, both cited above in chapter two, note 10.

[40]See the text quoted above from "Laws of Forbidden Intercourse," XIV 2.

[41]The Arabic has the singular.

[42]On this, see the discussion by Arthur Hyman in the article cited above in chapter two, note 1.

[43]On Joseph ben Judah ibn Shim'on see David Baneth, *Iggerot ha-Rambam* 2nd ed. (Jerusalem: Magnes Press, 1985), a collection of letters between Maimonides and Joseph and documents about Joseph. See also S. M. Stern, "A Collection of Treatises by Abd al-Latif al-Baghdadi," in his *Medieval Arabic and Hebrew Thought*, ed. F. W. Zimmermann (London: Variorum, 1983): 61. See further Twersky, *Introduction* (above, chapter two, note 10): 41-3.

[44]As noted above (note 41), Maimonides uses the singular here.

[45]For an excellent discussion of Maimonides' views on the perfection of the body, see Byron Sherwin, "Moses Maimonides on the Perfection of the Body," *Listening* 9 (1974): 28-37.

[46] *Contra* Miriam Galston, who makes the surprising assertion that "Maimonides never claims that theoretical perfection presupposes moral perfection. . . ." on p. 209 of her article, "Philosopher-King vs. Prophet," *Israel Oriental Studies* 7 (1978): 204-18. Further on the connection between moral and intellectual perfection in Maimonides, see pp. 459-60 in Henry Malter, "Shem Tob ben Joseph Palquera II: His 'Treatise of the Dream,'" *Jewish Quarterly Review* 1 (1910-11): 451-501. For yet another text which supports the interpretation presented here see *Guide* I 62 (p. 152).

[47]See Shem Tov, Efodi, Crescas, and Narboni *ad loc.* and the commentary of Yehudah Even-Shmuel in Vol. IV of his edition of the *Guide* (Jerusalem: Mossad ha-Rav Kook, 1987): 85-6. See also the two

studies by Ya'akov Levinger: *"Shelemut Enoshit Ezel ha-Goyyim li-fi ha-Rambam,"* Hagut II: Bein Yisrael la-Amim (Jerusalem: Ministry of Education, 1978): 27-36; *"Yihudo shel Yisrael, Arzo vi-Leshono li-fi ha-Rambam,"* Millet: Open University Studies in the History of Israel and its Culture (Tel Aviv: Open University, 1984): 289-97. See also Sara Klein-Braslavy, *Perush ha-Rambam la-Sippurim al Adam bi-Parashat Bereshit* (Jerusalem: Rubin Mass, 1986): 234-8.

[48] It is worthy of note that in III 53 (p. 631) Maimonides calls faith *(al-iman)* a moral virtue. I submit that it is extremely unlikely that Maimonides expected gentiles to have that particular virtue, making their overall moral perfection less likely and, therefore, their intellectual perfection less likely.

[49] See *Guide* I 54, p. 125.

[50] Maimonides himself can be faulted for giving legitimacy to this interpretation. See II 36.

[51] Compare Leo Strauss, *Philosophy and Law* (above, chapter two, note 1): 89-90. For a representative Maimonidean text (other than ones we are dealing with here), see "Laws of Repentance," X 3.

[52] This is important to him, I think, for reasons connected to his doctrine that in the days of the Messiah all human beings will achieve a very high level of perfection. See my article, "A Suggestion Concerning Maimonides' 'Thirteen Principles' and the Status of Non-Jews in the Messianic Era," in M. Ayali (ed.), *Tura: Oranim Studies in Honor of Simon Greenberg* (Tel Aviv: Ha-Kibbutz Ha-Meuhad, 1988): 249-260 (Hebrew).

[53] See Levinger, *Shelemut Enoshit,* cited above in note 47.

[54] As it must be, since it is one of the prerequisites of intellectual perfection, as noted above. For prophecy in particular, see "Laws of the Foundations of the Torah," VII 1, and *Guide* II 36 (p. 371).

[55] Hebrew (the Arabic original is lost): *da'ato.* Another possible translation is "his knowledge." On Maimonides' use of this term see David Baneth, *"La-Terminologiah ha-Philosophit shel ha-Rambam,"* Tarbiz 6 (1935): 254-84, p. 260; and David R. Blumenthal, "Maimonides on Mind and Metaphoric Language," in D. R. Blumenthal (ed.), *Approaches to Judaism in Medieval Times* II (Chico, California: Scholars Press, 1985): 123-32.

[56] The inconsistency between singular and plural is in the Hebrew.

[57]The letter was originally published in *Kovez Teshuvot ha-Rambam vi-Iggerotav* (Leipzig, 1859 [reprinted in Jerusalem in 1967]): 28, col. d. See also Alexander Marx, "Texts By and About Maimonides," *JQR* 25 (1934-5): 374-81. Alfred Ivry has recently explicated the letter in his "Islamic and Greek Influences on Maimonides' Philosophy," S. Pines and Y. Yovel (eds.), *Maimonides and Philosophy* (Dordrecht: Martinus Nijhoff, 1986): 139-56. See also Pines' translation of the letter in "Introduction," p. lix. Maimonides' comments on Aristotle here, it should be noted, drew the criticism of his great admirer, Shem Tov ibn Falaquera. See his "*Iggeret ha-Halom*," ed. by Henry Malter (above, note 46) p. 492.

[58]Even if one wishes to take Maimonides literally in the seventh of his "Thirteen Principles" (in the edition of Rabbi Kafih [above, chapter one, note 4], p. 212-14), where he asserts that Moses became more than human, he at least started out as a human being.

[59]Compare Abraham Joshua Heschel, "*Ha-He'emin ha-Rambam she-Zakhah li-Nevuah?*" in *Louis Ginzberg Jubilee Volume* (New York: American Academy for Jewish Research, 1946): 159-88. Heschel reads Maimonides as I do here on pp. 168-9. (My citing Heschel in this context does not mean that I accept without reservation his claims that Maimonides strove for prophetic inspiration himself and sought to guide the student for whom he wrote his work to actual prophecy.)

[60]See my *Dogma*: 41.

[61]As Maimonides writes: ." . . .the intellect which emanated from Him. . . .toward us is the bond between us and Him. You have the choice: if you wish to strengthen and fortify this bond, you can do so. . . .it is made weaker and feebler if you busy your thought with what is other than He" (III 51, p. 621). Maimonides seems to contradict this position at I 62 (p. 152); but see Berman's interpretation in his dissertation (above chapter two, note 4):   28-9. Compare also Sara Klein-Braslavy, *Perush ha-Rambam la-Sippurim al Adam bi-Parashat Bereshit* (Jerusalem: Rubin Mass, 1986): 257.

[62]On this "solitude" see Zvi (Harry) Blumberg, "*Al-Farabi, Ibn Bajja, vi-ha-Rambam al Hanhagat ha-Mitboded*," *Sinai* 78 (1976):   135-45. On worship in Maimonides (and on many of the issues taken up here), see Eliezer Goldman, "*Ha-Avodah ha-Meyuhedet shel Masig ha-Amitot*," *Bar Ilan University Annual* 6 (1968): 287-313 and Mosheh [Marvin] Fox, "*Ha-Tefilah bi-Mahshavto shel ha-Rambam*," in G. Cohen (ed.), *Ha-Tefilah ha-Yehudit — Hemshekh vi-Hiddush* (Ramat Gan: Bar Ilan University Press, 1978): 142-67.

[63]Moshe Idel goes so far as to say: "It was thus possible, according to Maimonides, to maintain the state of contemplation probably even during sexual intercourse." This high level of concentration, according to Idel, is not restricted to Moses and the Patriarchs but is something to which other individuals can and ought to aspire. See his "Sitre 'Arayot in Maimonides' Thought," in S. Pines and Y. Yovel (eds.), *Maimonides and Philosophy* (Dordrecht: Martinus Nijhoff, 1986): 79-91, p. 81. See also Howard (Haim) Kreisel, "Maimonides' View of Prophecy," *Da'at* 13 (1984): xxi-xxvi (English section), who interprets the relationship between contemplative and practical perfection thus: "Maimonides conceives of the final perfection in terms of descent from the mountain without leaving the summit, of governing others without ceasing to contemplate God" (p. xxiv).

[64]III 37 (p. 542). See also, p. 545 and "Laws of Idolatry," II 4.

[65]Compare *Book of Commandments*, positive commandment 3, where Maimonides tells us that love of God brings us to call others to belief in Him.

[66]See above, this chapter, note 8.

[67]This text is cited above fully in chapter one (at note 16).

[68]In a note to the text, Pines comments: "The Arabic phrase can have two meanings: (a) Someone like myself cannot aspire to be guided with a view to achieving this rank; (b) Someone like myself cannot aspire to guide others with a view to their achieving this rank." Both possibilities are consistent with my interpretation of the concluding exhortation.

[69]For example: who is the "king" mentioned at the beginning of the chapter? It would make sense to assume that Maimonides is continuing the parable developed in the previous chapter and interpret the king here as God. But Maimonides then says that this king is the intellect binding us to God and exposing us to His inspection. Shem Tov and Efodi, *ad loc.*, and Eliezer Goldman (see above, note 62), note 11, all suggest that the king is the Active Intellect. If this is the case, should we then read the parable in this fashion and interpret it as teaching that knowledge of God is impossible, but knowledge of the Active Intellect is not and is the highest level of human perfection? Second, Maimonides claims to *demonstrate* in this chapter that the end of the Law is the inculcation of the love and fear of God. Now, he certainly *asserts* this claim in the chapter, but nowhere *proves* it.

[70]On the superiority of doctrine over practice, see III 27 (p. 510), cited above; on the superiority of love of God over fear of God, see Maimonides' Introduction to *Helek* (in Rabbi Kafih's edition [above,

chapter one, note 4], p. 199) and "Laws of Repentance," chapter ten (passim).

[71]On the love of God finding expression in the fulfillment of the commandments, see Guide III 44 (p. 574), "Laws of the Lulav," VIII 15, "Laws of Repentance," X 2, the end of the fifth of the "Eight Chapters" (in the edition of Weiss and Butterworth [above, chapter one, note 4], p. 78), and Twersky, Introduction (above, chapter 2, note 10): 363.

[72]On the esoteric philosophical tradition referred to here, see Guide III, Introduction (p. 415) and I 71 (p. 175) along with the sources cited in my Dogma, p. 234 (note 169). To these should be added Shalom Rosenberg, "Al Parshanut ha-Mikra bi-Sefer ha-Moreh," Jerusalem Studies in Jewish Thought 1 (1981): 94n and 94-8.

[73]Arabic: fiqh. See Guide, Introduction (p. 5); Leo Strauss,"The Literary Character of the Guide of the Perplexed" (above, chapter two, note 1): 38; and my "The Conception of Torah as a Deductive Science in Medieval Jewish Thought," in Revue des etudes juives 146 (1987): 265-79.

[74]See Twersky's Introduction to the Code of Maimonides (above, chapter two, note 10): 362-3.

[75]See Guide, Introduction, pp. 8-9.

[76]On this text see Altmann's "Maimonides' 'Four Perfections,'" above, chapter one, note 20, and Norbert Samuelson's illuminating comments in his review of Altmann's Essays in Jewish Intellectual History in Modern Judaism 5 (1985): 191-6.

[77]I made use here of the index of biblical citations in Maimonides compiled by Rabbi J. Kafih: Ha-Mikra ba-Rambam (Jerusalem: Mossad ha-Rav Kook, n.d.).

[78]For a list of medieval and modern interpreters of Maimonides who maintain that he denied creation ex nihilo, see my Dogma, p. 242 (note 223). To that list should be added L. V. Berman in chapter three of his dissertation (see above, chapter two, note 4). On the question of providence in Maimonides, see Abraham Nuriel, "Hashgahah vi-Hanhagah bi-Moreh Nevukhim," Tarbiz 49 (1980): 346-55, and the recent study by Raffel (above, chapter two, note 1).

[79]See Berman's dissertation (above, chapter two, note 4): 37. Berman distinguishes between an ethical imitatio Dei before intellectual perfection and a political imitatio Dei after intellectual perfection.

Chapter Four

[1] *Theaetetus* 176 (in the edition of Benjamin Jowett [New York: Random House, 1937] II, p. 178). Compare *Laws* IV, 716 (Jowett, p. 488).

[2] See in particular, "The Political Interpretation of the Maxim: The Purpose of Philosophy is the Imitation of God," *Studia Islamica* 15 (1961): 53-61, and "Maimonides, the Disciple of Alfarabi," *Israel Oriental Studies* 4 (1974): 154-178, esp. note 57 (p. 171). See also Pines, "Introduction," p. xci.

[3] My thanks to Rabbi Dr. Tzvi Blanchard for suggesting this thought to me.

[4] On the imitation of God in Judaism, see Martin Buber, "Imitatio Dei," in Menachem M. Kellner (ed.), *Contemporary Jewish Ethics* (New York: Sanhedrin Press, 1978): 152-61; David S. Shapiro, "The Doctrine of the Image of God and *Imitatio Dei*," in *Contemporary Jewish Ethics*: 127-51; Louis Jacobs, Introduction to his translation of Moses Cordevero's *Palm Tree of Deborah* (New York: Sepher-Hermon Press, 1974): 18-20; and Harry Austryn Wolfson, *Philo*, 3rd ed. rev. (Cambridge: Harvard University Press, 1962), II: 194-6. Note should be made here of the fact that the term "halakhah" probably does not actually derive from the root "halakh," despite the indication to that effect at the end of Tractate Nidah (73a). See Saul Lieberman, *Hellenism in Jewish Palestine* (New York: Jewish Theological Seminary, 1950), p. 83, note 3.

[5] Actually, Maimonides appears to be wrong here. The passage in question is in fact a comment on Deut. 11:22 (which also includes the expression, *walk in all His ways*), not Deut. 10:12. See *Sifri ad loc.* A fair amount of confusion has been caused by this mistake as can be seen by examining the notes of the various editions of the *Book of Commandments.*

[6] Cited with emendations from the translation of Charles B. Chavel, *The Commandments: Sefer ha-Mizvoth of Maimonides* (London: Soncino, 1967), I: 11-12.

[7] As do many other halakhic decisors. See Shapiro (above, note 4), p. 148, note 69.

[8]How one imitates God by becoming like Him, as will be discussed below, depends upon one's conception of God. Imitating Aristotle's god, for example, involves one in the never-ending quest for ever greater intellectual perfection so as to become as much as possible an intellect like God.

[9]It is safe to assume that Maimonides followed in the footsteps of the Sages and did not see *all* of God's attributes as fit objects of imitation for all people. See Shapiro (above, note 4), pp. 130-5.

[10]I 6 (Hymason [above chapter one, note 6], pp. 47b-48a). For an important commentary on this passage, which shows that Maimonides did not intend to reduce *imitatio Dei* to some variant of Aristotle's middle way, see Schwarzschild (above, chapter two, note 3), pp. 68-9. Further on *imitatio Dei* in Maimonides, see Zvi (Harry) Blumberg, *"Musag ha-Razon ha-Elohi bi-Mishnato shel ha-Rambam,"* *Perakim* 4 (1966): 43-55, esp. p. 52; and Avraham Nuriel, *"Ha-Razon ha-Elohi bi-Moreh Nevukhim,"* *Tarbiz* 39 (1969): 39-61, esp. pp. 55-8.

[11]I have checked the references in Aaron Hyman, *Sefer Torah ha-Ketubah vi-ha-Mesurah*, 2nd ed. (Tel Aviv: Dvir, 1979), and in the companion volume, *Sefer ha-Hashlamot* (Jerusalem: Makhon Peri ha-Arez, 1985).

[12]See Chavel (above, note 6), II p. 380.

[13]Compare also I 69 (p. 170).

[14]Thus, for example, Deut. 28:9: . . .*if thou shalt keep the commandments of the Lord thy God and walk in His ways.* Compare also *Book of Commandments*, positive commandments 6 and 8, and "Laws of Moral Qualities," VI 2.

[15]See, for example, Maimonides' comments after the "Thirteen Principles" in Kafih (see above, chapter one, note 4), p. 217. Compare also the comments of Isadore Twersky, *Introduction* (above, chapter two, note 10), pp. 346-55, and the sources cited above in chapter three, note 29.

Chapter Five

[1]See above, chapter two, note 3.

[2]Maimonides would reject the name "morality" for the practical perfection which is to be sought after intellectual perfection for the simple reason that he himself reserves the term "morality" for a species of perfection which is inferior to intellectual perfection. This is evident from texts which we discuss here (including the "four perfections" of III 54 and the way in which immortality is always keyed to what Maimonides himself *calls* intellectual perfection, never what he *calls* moral perfection; thus, even if Schwarzschild means to claim that there is a moral side or expression to what Maimonides calls intellectual perfection, the terminological problem remains) and others. I cite two: (a) In the second of his *Eight Chapters*, Maimonides says that "the moral virtues are found only in the appetitive part [of the soul]" (in Weiss and Butterworth [see above, chapter one, note 4], p. 65); this is opposed to "the rational virtues which are found in the rational part [of the soul]." (b) In the seventh chapter, Maimonides says (p. 81) "that no prophet prophesies until after he acquires *all* the rational virtues and *most* of the moral virtues, i.e., the most important ones" [emphasis added]. In general, Cohen, Guttmann, and Schwarzschild would have us read Maimonides in an esoteric fashion, one which has him depreciating the value of morality with respect to intellectual perfection in public while prizing the former over the latter in private. But why keep such a doctrine secret? Cohen and Guttmann are guilty of what may be called an essential misrepresentation of Maimonides while Schwarzschild, who admits in effect that morality = halakhah, is merely guilty of using inappropriate terminology in describing the ultimately practical end of human perfection. Given contemporary realities (especially the way the ritual, *bein adam la-Makom*, aspect of halakhah is emphasized over *bein adam li-havero*), I have great sympathy for what Schwarzschild is trying to do. But I still think that one ought to call a spade a spade and try to distinguish between polemics (even polemics with which I agree!) and historical exposition.

[3]See Schwarzschild, p. 69.

[4]See Pines, "Translator's Introduction," p. cxxii, and his comments in "Spinoza's *Tractatus Theologico-Politicus*, Maimonides, and Kant," *Scripta Hierosolymitana* 20 (1968): 27-8.

[5]Schwarzschild does not document this claim. This is not surprising. I don't think that it can be documented. See also Eliezer Goldman (above, chapter three, note 62), p. 305.

[6]For a discussion of what might be considered some of God's "less attractive" features, see *Guide*, I 54. For further criticism of the moral interpretation of practical perfection, see Leo Strauss, "Maimonides' Statement on Political Science:" (above, chapter three, note 2), p. 127. For a discussion of the meaning of "wily deceit," see Amos Funkenstein, *Teva, Historiah, u-Meshihiut ezel ha-Rambam* (Tel Aviv: Ministry of Defense, 1983): 34-38.

[7]This is not the place for a full-scale exposition of my reasons for rejecting the radical naturalistic (or in modern terms, secularist) reading of Maimonides. Suffice it to say that with such a reading of Maimonides, it is difficult to make sense of the facts of his life as we know them unless we wanted to say that he suffered from a seriously split personality. For illuminating comments on the subject, see Twersky, *Introduction* (above, chapter two, note 10): 507-14. See also note 10 below.

[8]See Harry Austryn Wolfson, *The Philosophy of Spinoza* (Cambridge: Harvard University Press, 1934), I: 3. Wolfson himself is aware of the fact that philosophers are more than the sum total of their sources, since these sources are reshaped by the philosophers.

[9]Cited above, chapter two, note 4; see p. 155.

[10]I am grateful to Yizhak Gross for suggesting this to me. For an interesting and instructive parallel, see Ralph Lerner's criticism of Richard Walzer's reading of Al-Farabi in "Beating the Neoplatonic Bushes," *Journal of Religion* 67 (1987): 510-17, p. 516 (a review of the Walzer volume cited below in note 14). Alfred Ivry provides a brief biography of Maimonides which serves as a corrective to Berman's approach. See above, chapter three, note 57. The following articles on Maimonides' activities may be consulted with profit, as well: S. D. Goitein, "Moses Maimonides, Man of Action: A Revision of the Master's Biography in the Light of Genizah Documents," in G. Nahon and C. Touati (eds.), *Hommage A Georges Vajda* (Louvain: Deeters, 1980): 155-67; and Paul B. Fenton, "A Meeting With Maimonides," *Bulletin of the School of Oriental and African Studies* 45 (1982): 1-5.

[11]See above, chapter two, note 4.

[12]P. 118; emphasis added. This emphasis on the importance of *founding* a state is found in all of Berman's writings on the subject. See, for example, his dissertation, p. 23, and his "Political Interpretation of the Maxim. . .," p. 56 (both cited in chapter two, note 4). See also Pines, "Translator's Introduction," pp. cxxxi-cxxxii, and Leo Strauss, *Philosophy and Law* (above, chapter two, note 1), p. 53.

[13]Quoted by Fazlur Rahman, *Prophecy in Islam: Philosophy and Orthodoxy* (London: Allen and Unwin, 1958): 57. See Berman's discussion of the issue, and the texts he cites from Al-Farabi, in his dissertation (above, chapter two, note 4), chapter one. For a discussion of this text, which supports Rahman's interpretation, see Berman's "The Political Interpretation of the Maxim. . .," p. 58 (above, chapter two, note 4). Al-Farabi's statement quoted here is from his "Attainment of Happiness," translated by Muhsin Mahdi in *Alfarabi's Philosophy of Plato and Aristotle* (Ithaca: Cornell University Press, 1969). The passage in question is on p. 47.

[14]See Richard Walzer, *Alfarabi on the Perfect State* (Oxford: Clarendon Press, 1985). For a study linking Maimonides and this text and which interprets him in the spirit of Berman, *et al.*, see Joel Kraemer, "Alfarabi's *Opinions of the Virtuous City* and Maimonides' *Foundations of the Law*," in J. Blau, *et al.*, (eds.), *Studia Orientalia, Memoriae D. H. Baneth Dedicata* (Jerusalem: Magnes Press, 1979): 107-53. Kraemer's thesis is that Maimonides saw *himself* as a philosopher-statesman in the Al-Farabian mold, promulgating correct opinions for the citizens of the virtuous city. Compare the conclusion to Berman's "Maimonides, the Disciple of Alfarabi."

[15]See, for example, Ann K. S. Lambton, *State and Government in Medieval Islam* (Oxford: Oxford University Press, 1981).

[16]To cite just one example, see the biography of Averroes in Barry Kogan, *Averroes and the Metaphysics of Causation* (Albany: SUNY Press, 1985): 9-13.

[17]See Rahman (above, note 13), p. 109.

[18]For a statement typical of rabbinic views on the subject, see the attitude of the Sages toward Mordecai in Megillah 16b. For an alternative view of Jewish history, see David Biale's provocative study, *Power and Powerlessness in Jewish History* (New York: Schocken, 1986).

[19]Compare, for example, the assertion of Raymond L. Weiss in "The Adaptation of Philosophic Ethics to a Religious Community: Maimonides' *Eight Chapters*," *PAAJR* 54 (1987): 261-87: "the position of the Jews in the Diaspora obviously differs from the political independence taken for granted by Aristotle's discussion of ethics or, for that matter, by Alfarabi in his political works" (p. 272). A propos of Berman's reading of Maimonides, Weiss' following observation is worthy of note: ." . .the way in which Maimonides makes use of Alfarabi's *Selected Chapters*, an important source of the philosophic passages of *Eight Chapters*. The purpose of Alfarabi's work is to instruct a king or statesman; Maimonides

excises the political content from the passages incorporated into *Eight Chapters*" (p. 276); see also p. 271.

[20]This is indicated by the following: In II 36 (p. 369), Maimonides defines prophecy as follows: "Know that the true reality and essence of prophecy consists of its being an emanation emanating from God, may He be cherished and honored, through the intermediation of the Active Intellect, toward the rational faculty in the first place and thereafter toward the imaginative faculty." In the very same chapter (p. 373), Maimonides says of Moses that "the imaginative faculty did not enter into his prophecy." So, whatever Moses is, he does not fall under the definition of prophecy which Maimonides himself puts forward. See further "Laws of the Foundations of the Torah," VII, and the seventh of Maimonides' "Thirteen Principles."

[21]If the traditional reading of the parable is correct, then the person who imitates God does not even have to have Talmudic training, which training might be thought to be helpful to the legislator and statesman.

[22]See the texts cited above in note 20 and the following studies: Menachem Marc Kellner, "Maimonides and Gersonides on Mosaic Prophecy," *Speculum* 42 (1977): 62-79; D. R. Blumenthal's article cited above in chapter one, note 20; and Kalman Bland, "Moses and the Law According to Maimonides," in J. Reinharz and D. Swetschinsky (eds.), *Mystics, Philosophers and Politicians: Essays in Jewish Intellectual History in Honor of Alexander Altmann* (Durham: Duke University Press, 1982): 49-66.

[23]"Disciple," p. 168. Let it be noted that Maimonides nowhere "intimates that were Moses to come in his time," etc. The possibility of there being a "second Moses" is something Maimonides takes great pains to deny. To see in Maimonides' comments about the growing maturity of the human race and the concomitant dispensability of sacrifices an "intimation" of the doctrine of a second Moses is a violation of all canons of reasonable interpretation. On Maimonides' arguments against the notion of a second Moses, see the studies cited in the previous note.

[24]For further criticism of this approach to Maimonides, see Herbert A. Davidson, "Maimonides' *Shemonah Perakim* and Alfarabi's *Fusul al-Madani*," *PAAJR* 31 (1963): 33-50, esp. pp. 47-50 and most especially p. 49. Given that Davidson takes pains to show Maimonides' dependence upon Al-Farabi, his rejection of the approach criticized here takes on added significance.

Chapter Six

[1]On the need for the love of God to be wholly disinterested, with no anticipation of reward, see Maimonides' commentary on *Helek* (above, chapter one, note 4), p. 199, and "Laws of Repentance," X 1-2, 4-5.

[2]For other views on the connection between intellectual perfection and *imitatio Dei*, see Warren Zev Harvey, "*Bein Philosophiah Medinit vi-Halakhah bi-Mishnat ha-Rambam,*" *Iyyun* 29 (1980): 198-212 (appendix), and Haim (Howard) Kreisel, "*Hakham vi-Navi bi-Mishnat ha-Rambam Uvnei Hugo,*" *Eshel Beersheva* 3 (1986): 149-69.

[3]Maimonides takes with ultimate seriousness the mishnaic statement, *sekhar mizvah, mizvah*: "the reward of a commandment is another commandment." See Avot IV 2.

Chapter Seven

[1]See his "Translator's Introduction," p. xcvii, his article on Maimonides in the *Encyclopedia of Philosophy* (above, chapter three, note 15): 131, and his article on "Jewish Philosophy," in the 15th edition of the *Encyclopaedia Britannica*, Vol. 10: 211-2.

[2]"Introduction," p. xcviii.

[3]See "Introduction," p. xcviii, and Pines' article in the *Encyclopedia of Philosophy* (above, chapter three, note 15): 131.

[4]Shlomo Pines shows the Aristotelian roots of the equation knowing = knower = known on p. xcviii of "Introduction." See also Harry Austryn Wolfson, "The Knowability and Describability of God in Plato and Aristotle," *Harvard Studies in Classical Philology* 56-57 (1947): 233-49, reprinted in Wolfson, *Studies in the History of Philosophy and Religion*, Vol. I (Cambridge: Harvard University Press, 1973): 98-114.

[5]See Harry Austryn Wolfson, *Philo*, 3rd ed. rev. (Cambridge: Harvard University Press, 1962), Vol. II: 118-26 and 158-60.

[6]Quoted by Harry Austryn Wolfson, *Philo* (see previous note), Vol. I: 295.

Chapter Eight

[1]The situation may be even more complicated if Sara Klein-Braslavy is right and Maimonides himself could not make up his mind about some of the issues which he raised in the *Guide*. See her "The Creation of the World and Maimonides' Interpretation of Genesis i-iv," in S. Pines and Y. Yovel (eds.), *Maimonides and Philosophy* (Dordrecht: Martinus Nijhoff, 1986): 65-78.

Bibliography

Abravanel, Isaac. *Haslat Abravanel–Ma'amar Kazar bi-Veur Sod ha-Moreh* (Venice, 1574). Reprinted in Don Isaac Abravanel, *Opera Minora* (Westmead: Gregg International, 1972).

Altmann, Alexander. "Maimonides' 'Four Perfections'," *Israel Oriental Studies* 2 (1972): 15-24. Reprinted with additions in Altmann, *Essays in Jewish Intellectual History* (Hanover [N.H.]: University Press of New England, 1981): 65-76.

———. "Maimonides on the Intellect and the Scope of Metaphysics," in Altmann, *Von der mittelalterlichen zur modernen Aufklaerung* (Tuebingen: JCB Mohr, 1986): 60-129.

Baneth, David. "La-Terminologiah ha-Philosophit shel ha-Rambam," *Tarbiz* 6 (1935): 254-84. Reprinted in *Likkutei Tarbiz 5: Mikra'ah bi-Heker ha-Rambam* (Jerusalem: Magnes Press, 1985): 10-40.

Berman, Lawrence V. "Ibn Bajjah vi-ha-Rambam" Ph.D. Diss.; Hebrew University of Jerusalem, 1959.

———. "Maimonides on the Fall of Man," *AJS Review* 5 (1980): 1-15.

———. "Maimonides on Political Leadership," Daniel J. Elazar (ed.), *Kinship and Consent* (Ramat Gan: Turtledove, 1981): 13-25.

———. "Maimonides, the Disciple of Alfarabi," *Israel Oriental Studies* 4 (1974): 154-78.

———. "The Political Interpretation of the Maxim: The Purpose of Philosophy Is the Imitation of God," *Studia Islamica* 15 (1961): 53-61.

———. "A Re-examination of Maimonides' Statement on Political Science," *Journal of the American Oriental Society* 89 (1969): 106-111.

———. "Some Remarks on the Arabic Text of Maimonides' 'Treatise on the Art of Logic,'" *Journal of the American Oriental Society* 88 (1968): 340-2.

———. "The Structure of Maimonides' *Guide of the Perplexed*," *Proceedings of the Sixth World Congress of Jewish Studies* III (Jerusalem: World Union of Jewish Studies, 1977): 7-17.

Biale, David. *Power and Powerlessness in Jewish History* (New York: Schocken, 1986).

Bland, Kalman. "Moses and the Law According to Maimonides," J. Reinharz and D. Swetschinsky (eds.), *Mystics, Philosophers, and Politicians: Essays in Jewish Intellectual History in Honor of Alexander Altmann* (Durham: Duke University Press, 1982): 49-66.

Blumberg, Zvi (Harry). "Al-Farabi, ibn Bajjah vi-ha-Rambam al Hanhagat ha-Mitboded," *Sinai* 78 (1976): 35-45.

———. "Ha-Sekhalim ha-Nivdalim bi-Mishnato shel ha-Rambam," *Tarbiz* 40 (1971): 216-25.

———. "Musag ha-Razon ha-Elohi bi-Mishnato shel ha-Rambam," *Perakim* 4 (1966): 43-55.

——. "The Problem of Immortality in Avicenna, Maimonides and St. Thomas Aquinas," *Harry Austryn Wolfson Jubilee Volume* (Jerusalem: American Academy for Jewish Research, 1965): 165-85. Reprinted in Jacob I. Dienstag (ed.), *Studies in Maimonides and St. Thomas Aquinas* (New York: Ktav, 1975): 29-49.

Blumenthal, David R. *The Commentary of R. Hoter ben Shelomoh to the Thirteen Principles of Maimonides* (Leiden: Brill, 1974).

——. "Maimonides' Intellectualist Mysticism and the Superiority of the Prophecy of Moses," *Studies in Medieval Culture* 10 (1978): 51-67.

——. "Maimonides on Mind and Metaphoric Language," D. R. Blumenthal (ed.), *Approaches to Judaism in Medieval Times*, Vol. II (Chico, California: Scholars Press, 1985): 123-32.

Buber, Martin. "Imitatio Dei," M. Kellner (ed.), *Contemporary Jewish Ethics* (New York: Sanhedrin Press, 1978): 152-61.

Buijs, Joseph. "The Philosophical Character of Maimonides' *Guide* – A Critique of Strauss' Interpretation," *Judaism* 27 (1978): 448-57.

Butterworth, Charles. "On Scholarship and Scholarly Conventions," *Journal of the American Oriental Society* 106 (1986): 725-32.

Cohen, Hermann. "*Ofyah shel Torat ha-Middot li-ha-Rambam*," in H. Cohen, *Iyyunim bi-Yahadut u-vi-Ba'ayot ha-Dor* (Jerusalem: Mossad Bialik, 1978): 17-59.

Davidson, Herbert A. "Maimonides' *Shemonah Perakim* and Alfarabi's *Fusul al-Madani*," *Proceedings of the American Academy for Jewish Research* 31 (1963): 47-50.

——. "The Middle Way in Maimonides' Ethics," *Proceedings of the American Academy for Jewish Research* 54 (1987): 31-72.

Diesendruck, Zvi. "Die Teleologie bei Maimonides," *Hebrew Union College Annual* 5 (1928): 415-535.

——. "*Ha-Takhlit vi-ha-Toarim bi-Torat ha-Rambam*," *Tarbiz* 1 (1930): 106-36; and 2 (1931): 27-73. Reprinted in *Likkutei Tarbiz 5: Mikra'ah bi-Heker ha-Rambam* (Jerusalem: Magnes Press, 1985): 187-264.

——. "Samuel and Moses ibn Tibbon on Maimonides' Theory of Providence," *Hebrew Union College Annual* 11 (1936): 341-66.

Drury, S. B. "The Esoteric Philosophy of Leo Strauss," *Political Theory* 13 (1985): 315-37.

Duran, Profiat (Efodi). *Commentary on the Guide of the Perplexed* (Vilna, 1904).

Feldman, Seymour. "Introduction" to *Levi ben Gershom, Wars of the Lord*, Vol. 1 (Philadelphia: Jewish Publication Society, 1984).

Fenton, Paul B. "A Meeting with Maimonides," *Bulletin of the School of Oriental and African Studies* 45 (1982): 1-5.

Fox, Marvin. "A New View of Maimonides' Method of Contradictions," *Bar Ilan: Annual of Bar Ilan University – Studies in Judaica and Humanities* 22-23 (Moshe Schwarcz Memorial Volume) (Ramat Gan: Bar Ilan University Press, 1987): 19-43.

——. "Ha-Tefilah bi-Mahshavto shel ha-Rambam," G. Cohen (ed.), Ha-Tefilah ha-Yehudit–Hemshekh vi-Hiddush (Ramat Gan: Bar Ilan University Press, 1978): 142-67.

Frank, Daniel H. "The End of the Guide: Maimonides on the Best Life for Man," Judaism 34 (1985): 485-95.

Funkenstein, Amos. Teva, Historiah u-Meshihut ezel ha-Rambam (Tel Aviv: Ministry of Defense, 1983).

Galston, Miriam. "Philosopher-King vs. Prophet," Israel Oriental Studies 7 (1978): 204-18.

Goitein, S. D. "Moses Maimonides: Man of Action – A Revision of the Master's Biography in the Light of Genizah Documents," G. Nahon and C. Touati (eds.), Hommage a Georges Vajda (Louvain: Deeters, 1980): 155-67.

Goldman, Eliezer. "Ha-Avodah ha-Meyuhedet shel Masig ha-Amitot," Bar Ilan: Annual of Bar Ilan University 6 (Ramat Gan: Bar Ilan University Press, 1968): 287-313.

Guttmann, Julius. "Introduction and Commentary" to Moses Maimonides, Guide of the Perplexed: An Abridged Edition, translated by Chaim Rabin (London: East and West Library, 1947).

——. Philosophies of Judaism (New York: Schocken Books, 1973).

Hartman, David. Maimonides: Torah and Philosophic Quest (Philadelphia: Jewish Publication Society, 1976).

Harvey, Warren Zev. "Bein Philosophiah Medinit li-Halakhah bi-Mishnat ha-Rambam," Iyyun 29 (1980): 198-212.

——. "Hasdai Crescas' Critique of the Theory of the Acquired Intellect" Ph.D. Diss., (Columbia University, 1973).

——. "R. Hasdai Crescas u-Vikorto al ha-Osher ha-Philosophi," Proceedings of the Sixth World Congress of Jewish Studies III (Jerusalem: World Congress of Jewish Studies, 1977): 143-9.

——. "The Return of Maimonideanism," Journal of Jewish Social Studies 42 (1980): 249-68.

Heller, Joseph. "Mahuto vi-Tafkido shel ha-Sekhel ha-Poel lifi Torat ha-Rambam," S. Bernstein and G. Churgin (eds.), S. K. Mirsky Jubilee Volume (New York, 1958): 26-42.

Heschel, Abraham Joshua. "Ha-He'emin ha-Rambam she-Zakhah li-Nevuah?" Louis Ginzberg Jubilee Volume (New York: American Academy for Jewish Research, 1946): 159-88.

Husik, Isaac. A History of Medieval Jewish Philosophy (New York: Macmillan, 1930).

Hyman, Aaron. Sefer ha-Torah ha-Ketubah vi-ha-Mesurah, 2nd ed. (Tel Aviv: Dvir, 1979).

Hyman, Arthur. "Interpreting Maimonides," Gesher 5 (1976): 46-59.

Hyman, Dov. Sefer ha-Hashlamot li-Hibbur Torah ha-Ketubah vi-ha-Mesurah (Jerusalem: Makhon Peri ha-Arez, 1985).

Ibn Falaquera, Shem Tov. Moreh ha-Moreh (Pressburg, 1837). Reprinted in Sheloshah Kadmonei Meforshei ha-Moreh (Jerusalem, 1961).

Idel, Moshe. *The Mystical Experience in Abraham Abulafia* (Albany: SUNY Press, 1988).

———. "Sitre Arayot in Maimonides' Thought," S. Pines and Y. Yovel (eds.), *Maimonides and Philosophy* (Dordrecht: Martinus Nijhoff, 1986): 79-91.

Ivry, Alfred. "Islamic and Greek Influences on Maimonides' Philosophy," S. Pines and Y. Yovel (eds.), *Maimonides and Philosophy* (Dordrecht: Martinus Nijhoff, 1986): 139-56.

Jacobs, Louis, "Introduction" to Moses Cordevero, *Palm Tree of Deborah* (New York: Sepher Hermon-Press, 1974).

Jospe, Raphael. "Rejecting Moral Virtue as the Ultimate End," William Brinner and Stephen Ricks (eds.), *Studies in Islamic and Jewish Traditions* (Denver: University of Denver, 1986): 185-204.

Kafih, Joseph. *Ha-Mikra ba-Rambam* (Jerusalem: Mossad ha-Rav Kook, n.d.).

Kasher, Hannah. "Maimonides' Philosophical Division of the Laws," *Hebrew Union College Annual* 56 (1985): 1-7 (Hebrew section).

Katz, Ya'akov. *Halakhah vi-Kabbalah* (Jerusalem: Magnes Press, 1974).

Kellner, Menachem. "A Suggestion Concerning Maimonides' 'Thirteen Principles' and the Status of Non-Jews in the Messianic Era," M. Ayali (ed.), *Tura: Oranim Studies in Honor of Simon Greenberg* (Tel Aviv: Ha-Kibbutz Ha-Meuhad, 1988): 249-260 (Hebrew).

———. "The Conception of Torah as a Deductive Science in Medieval Jewish Thought," *Revue des etudes juives* 146 (1987): 265-79.

———. *Dogma in Medieval Jewish Thought* (Oxford: Oxford University Press, 1986).

———. "Maimonides and Gersonides on Mosaic Prophecy," *Speculum* 42 (1977): 62-79.

———. "Maimonides' 'Thirteen Principles' and the Structure of the *Guide of the Perplexed*," *Journal for the History of Philosophy* 20 (1982): 76-84.

Klein-Braslavy, Sara, "The Creation of the World and Maimonides' Interpretation of Gen. i-iv," S. Pines and Y. Yovel (eds.), *Maimonides and Philosophy* (Dordrecht: Martinus Nijhoff, 1986): 65-78.

———. *Perush ha-Rambam la-Sippurim al Adam bi-Parashat Bereshit* (Jerusalem: Rubin Mass, 1986).

Kogan, Barry. *Averroes on the Metaphysics of Causation* (Albany: SUNY Press, 1985).

Kraemer, Joel. "Alfarabi's *Opinions of the Virtuous City* and Maimonides' Foundations of the Law," J. Blau, et al. (eds.), *Studia Orientalia, Memoriae D. H. Baneth Dedicata* (Jerusalem: Magnes Press, 1979): 107-53.

Kreisel, Haim (Howard). "*Hakham u-Navi bi-Mishnat ha-Rambam Uvnei Hugo*," *Eshel Beersheva* 3 (1986): 149-69.

———. "Maimonides' View of Prophecy," *Da'at* 13 (1984): xxi-xxvi.

———. "*Zaddik vi-Ra Lo ba-Philosophiah ha-Yehudit bimei ha-Benayim*," *Da'at* 19 (1987): 17-29.

Lambton, Ann K. S. *State and Government in Medieval Islam* (Oxford: Oxford University Press, 1981).

Leaman, Oliver, "Does the Interpretation of Islamic Philosophy Rest on a Mistake?" *International Journal of Middle East Studies* 12 (1980): 525-38.

——. *Introduction to Medieval Islamic Philosophy* (Cambridge: Cambridge University Press, 1985).

Lerner, Ralph. "Beating the Neoplatonic Bushes," *Journal of Religion* 67 (1987): 510-17.

Levinger, Ya'akov. *"Shelemut Enoshit Ezel ha-Goyyim lifi ha-Rambam,"* *Hagut II: Bein Yisrael la-Amim* (Jerusalem: Ministry of Education, 1978): 27-36.

——. *"Yihudo shel Yisrael, Arzo, vi-Leshono lifi ha-Rambam,"* *Millet: Open University Studies in the History of Israel and Its Culture* (Tel Aviv: Open University, 1984): 289-97.

Lieberman, Saul. *Hellenism in Jewish Palestine* (New York: Jewish Theological Seminary, 1950).

Maimonides, Moses. *Book of Commandments,* translated by Charles B. Chavel (London: Soncino, 1967).

——. *Book of Judges,* translated by A. M. Hershman (New Haven: Yale University Press, 1949).

——. *Book of Knowledge,* translated by Moses Hyamson (New York: Feldheim, 1974).

——. *Ethical Writings of Maimonides,* edited by Raymond L. Weiss and Charles Butterworth (New York: Dover, 1983).

——. *Iggerot ha-Rambam,* 2nd ed., edited and translated by David Baneth, (Jerusalem: Magnes Press, 1985).

——. *Iggerot ha-Rambam,* edited and translated by Joseph Kafih (Jerusalem: Mossad ha-Rav Kook, 1972).

——. *Guide of the Perplexed,* translated by Shlomo Pines (Chicago: University of Chicago Press, 1963).

——. *Kovez Teshuvot ha-Rambam vi-Iggerotav* (Leipzig, 1959; photo-reprinted in Jerusalem in 1967).

——. *Mishnah im Perush Rabbenu Mosheh ben Maimon,* edited and translated by Joseph Kafih (Jerusalem: Mossad ha-Rav Kook, 1963).

——. *Moreh Nevukhim,* Vol. IV, edited by Yehudah Even Shmuel, (Jerusalem: Mossad ha-Rav Kook, 1987).

——. *Pirkei Mosheh,* edited by S. Muntner (Jerusalem: Mossad ha-Rav Kook, 1959).

Malter, Henry. "Shem Tob ben Joseph Palquera II: His 'Treatise of the Dream,'" *Jewish Quarterly Review* 1 (1910-11): 451-501.

Marx, Alexander. "Texts By and About Maimonides," *Jewish Quarterly Review* 25 (1934-5): 374-81.

Melamed, Abraham. *"Al Yithalel–Perushim Philosophi'im li-Yirmiyahu 9: 22-23 ba-Mahshavah ha-Yehudit bi-Yimei ha-Benayim vi-ha-Renaissance,"* *Jerusalem Studies in Jewish Thought* 4 (1985): 31-82.

Motzkin, Aryeh Leo. "On the Interpretation of Maimonides," *International Journal of Philosophy* 2 (1978): 39-46.

Novak, David. *The Image of the Non-Jew in Judaism* (New York: Mellen, 1983).

Nuriel, Avraham. "*Ha-Razon ha-Elohi bi-Moreh Nevukhim,*" *Tarbiz* 39 (1969): 39-61.

———. "*Hashgahah vi-Hanhagah bi-Moreh Nevukhim,*" *Tarbiz* 49 (1980): 346-55.

Pines, Shlomo. "Abul-Barakat's Poetics and Metaphysics," *Scripta Hiersolymitana* 6 (1960): 120-98.

———. "Jewish Philosophy," *Encyclopaedia Britannica*, 15th ed., Vol. 10.

———. "The Limitations of Human Knowledge According to Al-Farabi, ibn Bajjah, and Maimonides," Isadore Twersky (ed.), *Studies in Medieval Jewish History and Literature* I (Cambridge: Harvard University Press, 1979): 82-109.

———. "Maimonides," *Encyclopedia of Philosophy*, Vol. 5 (New York: MacMillan, 1967).

———. "The Philosophic Purport of Maimonides' Halachic Works and the Purport of the *Guide of the Perplexed,*" S. Pines and Y. Yovel (eds.), *Maimonides and Philosophy* (Dordrecht: Martinus Nijhoff, 1986): 1-14.

———. "Spinoza's *Tractatus Theologico-Politicus*, Maimonides, and Kant," *Scripta Hierosolymitana* 20 (1968): 3-54.

———. "Translator's Introduction: The Philosophic Sources of the *Guide of the Perplexed,*" in *Guide of the Perplexed*, translated by Shlomo Pines (Chicago: University of Chicago Press, 1963).

Plato. *Laws*, translated by Benjamin Jowett (New York: Random House, 1937).

———. *Theaetetus*, translated by Benjamin Jowett (New York: Random House, 1937).

Raffel, Charles M. "Providence as Consequent Upon the Intellect: Maimonides' Theory of Providence," *AJS Review* 12 (1987): 25-71.

Rahman, Fazlur. *Prophecy in Islam: Philosophy and Orthodoxy* (London: Allen and Unwin, 1958).

Ravitzky, Aviezer. "Samuel ibn Tibbon and the Esoteric Character of *The Guide of the Perplexed,*" *AJS Review* 6 (1981): 87-123.

———. "*Sitrei Torato shel 'Moreh ha-Nevukhim':* *ha-Parshanut bi-Dorotav u-vi-Doroteinu,*" *Jerusalem Studies in Jewish Thought* 5 (1987): 23-69.

Rosenberg, Shalom. "*Al Parshanut ha-Mikra bi-Sefer ha-Moreh,*" *Jerusalem Studies in Jewish Thought* 1 (1981): 85-157.

———. "Ethics," Arthur A. Cohen and Paul Mendes-Flohr (eds.), *Contemporary Jewish Religious Thought* (New York: Scribners, 1987): 195-202.

Samuelson, Norbert M. "Review of Alexander Altmann, *Essays in Jewish Intellectual History,*" *Modern Judaism* 5 (1985): 191-6.

Schwarzschild, Steven S. "Do Noachites Have to Believe in Revelation?" *Jewish Quarterly Review* 52 (1962): 297-398; and 53 (1962): 30-65.

———. "Moral Radicalism and 'Middlingness' in the Ethics of Maimonides," *Studies in Medieval Culture* 11 (1977): 64-95.

Shapiro, David. "The Doctrine of the Image of God and *Imitatio Dei*," Menachem Kellner (ed.), *Contemporary Jewish Ethics* (New York: Sanhedrin Press, 1978): 127-51.

Shem Tov ben Joseph ibn Shem Tov. *Commentary on the Guide of the Perplexed* (Vilna, 1904).

Sherwin, Byron. "Moses Maimonides on the Perfection of the Body," *Listening* 9 (1974): 28-37.

Stern, Josef. "The Idea of a *Hoq* in Maimonides' Explanation of the Law," S. Pines and Y. Yovel (eds.), *Maimonides and Philosophy* (Dordrecht: Martinus Nijhoff, 1986): 92-130.

Stern, S. M. "A Collection of Treatises by Abd al-Latif al-Baghdadi," S. M. Stern, *Medieval Arabic and Hebrew Thought*, edited by F. W. Zimmermann (London: Variorum, 1983).

Strauss, Leo. "How to Begin to Study the *Guide of the Perplexed*," in Moses Maimonides, *Guide of the Perplexed*, translated by Shlomo Pines (Chicago: University of Chicago Press, 1963): xi-lvi.

———. "The Literary Character of the *Guide of the Perplexed*," S. W. Baron (ed.), *Essays on Maimonides* (New York: Columbia University Press, 1941): 37-91.

———. "Maimonides' Statement on Political Science," *Proceedings of the American Academy for Jewish Research* 22 (1953): 115-30.

———. *Persecution and the Art of Writing* (Glencoe, Illinois: Free Press, 1976).

———. *Philosophy and Law* (Philadelphia: Jewish Publication Society, 1987).

Twersky, Isadore. *Introduction to the Code of Maimonides* (New Haven: Yale University Press, 1980).

———. "Some Non-Halakic Aspects of the Mishneh Torah," A. Altmann (ed.), *Jewish Medieval and Renaissance Studies* (Cambridge: Harvard University Press, 1967): 161-82. Reprinted in Twersky, *Studies in Jewish Law and Philosophy* (New York: Ktav, 1982): 52-75.

Urbach, Ephraim E. *The Sages: Their Concepts and Beliefs* (Jerusalem: Magnes Press, 1975).

Vajda, Georges. *L'amour de Dieu dans la théologie juive du moyen âge* (Paris: Vrin, 1957).

Walzer, Richard. *Alfarabi on the Perfect State* (Oxford: Clarendon Press, 1985).

Weiss, Raymond L. "The Adaptation of Philosophic Ethics to a Religious Community: Maimonides' *Eight Chapters*," *Proceedings of the American Academy for Jewish Research* 54 (1987): 261-87.

Wolfson, Harry A. "The Knowability and Describability of God in Plato and Aristotle," *Harvard Studies in Classical Philology* 56-57 (1947): 233-49. Reprinted in H. A. Wolfson, *Studies in the History and Philosophy of Religion* Vol. I (Cambridge: Harvard University Press, 1973): 98-114.

——. *Philo*, 3rd ed. rev. (Cambridge: Harvard University Press, 1962).

——. *The Philosophy of the Church Fathers*, 3rd ed. rev. (Cambridge: Harvard University Press, 1970).

——. *The Philosophy of Spinoza* (Cambridge: Harvard University Press, 1934).

I. General Index

Aaron 4
Active Intellect 79
acquired intellect 2
Al-Farabi 9, 17, 39, 49, 50, 51, 52, 85
Amalek 18, 74
Aristotle 9, 17, 30, 39, 51, 59, 60, 61, 65, 78, 82

Berman, Lawrence 8, 9, 23, 34, 37, 38, 39, 41, 47, 49-52, 80, 84

Cohen, Hermann 8, 9, 41, 47, 48, 70, 83
creation 37, 80

Davidson, Herbert 86

Efodi (Profiat Duran) 15-16
esotericism 7, 68-9

faith 77

Galston, Miriam 76
God, attributes of action 29
God, imitation of 8, 9, 37, 38, 39, 41-45, 47, 50-53, 55-57, 59-60, 63-64,
80, 81, 82, 87
God, love of 29, 31, 32, 33, 34, 35, 39, 56, 67, 79, 80, 87
God, worship of 13, 14, 31, 32, 33, 78
Guide of the Perplexed, contradictions in 7
Guttmann, Julius 8, 9, 41, 47, 48, 70, 83

halakhists 14, 16, 17, 19, 20 (*see* Talmudists)
Halevi, Judah 30
Hartman, David 10, 47
Heschel, Abraham 78

Ibn Falaquera, Shem Tov 16
Ibn Shem Tov, Shem Tov ben Joseph 15
Ibn Tibbon, Samuel 30
immortality 1, 2, 3, 57

Jeremiah 7, 35, 36, 37
Joseph ben Judah 24-26, 76

Kafih, Joseph 23
Kant, Immanuel 41
Klein-Braslavi, Sara 88

II. Index of Passages

Bible

Exodus
33:1   36
33:5   36
33:12 36
33:13 36
34:28 15

Leviticus
19:2   42, 43, 44,

Deuteronomy
10:12 42
13:5   42
25:19 74
28:9   42, 82

Jeremiah
9:22-23 7

Psalms
16:3   16

Maimonides' Writings

Commentary on the Mishnah 1, 65

Book of Commandments 42

Mishneh Torah
Introduction 43, 75
"Laws of the Foundations of the Torah" I 6 22, IV 9 1
"Laws of Moral Qualities" 2, I 6 43
"Laws of Repentance" V 3 22, VIII 3 2
"Laws of the Reading of the Sh'ma" I 2 22
"Laws of Tefilin," VI 13 2
"Laws of Forbidden Intercourse" XIV 2 22
"Laws of Kings and their Wars" V 4 17, V 5 74, VIII 9 18, VIII 11 18

Guide of the Perplexed
Introduction 7, 70
I 1   55
I 2   3, 55

I 30   3
I 34   26-7
I 54   36, 43
I 68   59
II 30   28
II 36   86
III 8   3
III 24 34
III 27 4, 27, 28,
III 28 4
III 37 32
III 47 44
III 51 4, 5, 13, 14, 15, 18, 25-26, 29, 31, 32, 33, 78
III 52 33
III 53 34
III 54 5, 7-8, 8, 27, 34, 35, 36, 37, 88

Teshuvot 67

Brown Judaic Studies